BIRTH OF THE BLACK PANTHERS

152 (F) (Hyderabad) Squadron (Motto - Faithful Ally)

Great Britain
North Africa
Malta
Siciliy
Italy
India
Burma

William S. Smith

Published by

**MELROSE
BOOKS**

An Imprint of Melrose Press Limited
St Thomas Place, Ely
Cambridgeshire
CB7 4GG, UK
www.melrosebooks.co.uk

FIRST EDITION

Copyright © William S. Smith 2012

The Author asserts his moral right to
be identified as the author of this work

Cover designed by Teri Smith

ISBN   978-1-907732-86-7

Printed and bound in Great Britain by:
CPI Antony Rowe. Chippenham, Wiltshire

FSC
www.fsc.org
MIX
Paper from
responsible sources
FSC® C013604

This personal history of 152 "Hyderabad" F Squadron
Is dedicated to Ray Johnson "Sergeant Armourer"
Thank you Ray for your inspiration and support

Ray in Calcutta - December 1943
Taken soon after arriving in India from the Italian Campaign

RAF Coningsby at the 60th anniversary of The Battle of Britain
Ray beside Mk XIX Spitfire No PS915 from the BB Memorial Flight
Painted in the livery of the Black Panther to honour 152 (Hyderabad) (F) Sqdn

Contents

Foreword

It was at Duxford 1998, after corresponding with Bill Smith, that I eventually met up with him, his wife Mary and their two sons Teri and Barry. For me it was a very emotive occasion, Bill being the younger brother of Len, one of the six or seven most popular, skilful and successful pilots ever to grace 152 squadron.

To include Len's name and memory with that of Derek Boitel-Gill, Graham Cox, Boy Marrs, Dennis David, Birdie Wilson and Norman Jones must give some idea of the high esteem in which Smithy's memory is held by all who knew him.

With such illustrious company in mind I was extremely touched when asked if I would pen a forward to his book on the W.W.II history of no.152 Hyderabad Squadron.

After all, I was only a lowly armourer on the squadron for most of the war and therefore the only reason I can come up with is I spoke a few words into a hand held recorder so that at a future date someone would find the contents of interest.

Thank you Bill for allowing me the opportunity of penning these words in appreciation of your effort.

Ray Johnson
October 2001

The Beginning

Always interested in anything to do with flying, my attention was attracted one evening by a television programme called *The History of Powered Flight*. It was being introduced by a chap called Chabot (pronounced 'Shabo'). A very nice, short, rotund old gentleman with laughing eyes, and here he was sitting in the cockpit of a Blériot, one of the earliest aircraft produced. The year was about 1980, and Chabot (born in 1890) came across as a very lively ninety-year old. Among his many reminiscences that struck a chord was his sudden mention of No.152 Squadron; it would be most fortunate therefore that I decided to videotape his very absorbing programme for within three years dear Chabot had passed away and I could have lost his contribution to my 2001 endeavour forever.

As part of the military stationed at Bangkok, news reached him that the First World War had broken out, but being a bit far flung so to speak, he and his compatriots put the concept out of their minds until the following day. After that things began hotting up because any types able to assist in the performance of war were quickly mobilised for the return home.

Chabot tells of travelling through the Suez Canal and hearing this throbbing sound above his head. With all eyes on deck now peering skywards, for the first time Chabot saw a flying machine, a string and canvas biplane, in all probability an early Box Kite.

What a way to travel, he thought, I must look into this flying lark!!

I followed his programme with fascination: how, when trying to get into the Royal Flying Corps he was told you had to be at least a Guards officer, which clearly he was not. Then an acquaintance confided that he'd overheard a chap remark one day, that if you could fly and had a ticket you could join something known as the Special Reserve.

At that time you could pop down to Brooklands in Surrey, have a chat with the flight instructors and for a few bob book yourself a lesson. This so called lesson comprised clambering aboard a Longhorn biplane, which sported a long skid in front to save the thing from tipping onto its nose, then having to reach over the instructor's shoulders to grab the controls and literally fly the thing from the back seat.

Amazingly after only fifty minutes of this loosely termed tuition the instructor said you might as well try it by yourself now! Which good old Chabot did without trouble! After that he was told, 'If you can give me five figures of eight, and fly her to one thousand feet you can earn your ticket.'

With a little foresight, a few bob, and a measure of good fortune, our young Chabot had launched himself into the RFC.

His adventures are a book in themselves, but for my purposes it was his actual mention of 152 that made me sit up and take notice. This was a squadron comprising Sopwith Camel night fighters formed on the 1st June 1918 at Rochford in Essex. They were needed to help thwart enemy bombing raids against our bases, and to this end found themselves at Carvin in France by mid-October.

It was three weeks to war's end and Chabot had been scheduled to patrol as dusk fell. Sometime after take off he suffered a complete engine failure at 4000 feet, forcing him to find a suitable spot in which to put her down.

Light had faded fast and without the airfield flare markers which would normally have guided him in, he had to think fast. The only way, he reasoned, was to literally keep on landing, pulling back on the controls until she stalled and then try again and again, until suddenly she touched and rolled to a standstill.

Clambering out, immediately he began falling over barbed wire and sliding into shell holes, in the process hurting himself quite badly, until giving up the struggle he decided to retrace his steps back to the Camel, but so intense had the darkness become he was now unable to locate his machine. When daylight did eventually break, to his amazement he found he had touched down on the only decent patch of flat undamaged land as far as the eye could see.

The squadron would be disbanded on the 30th June 1919, but with the advent of the Second World War be reformed one month after the declaration on the 1st October 1939.

A squadron consists of all those who serve in it throughout its history, but it is not always possible to name and thereby honour everyone. Our colourful Chabot deserves to be our first introduction to this particular squadron.

There are many famous squadrons, and no doubt some with greater distinction when operating against the enemy, but 152 does have claim to some uniqueness. It flew from October 1939 to September 1945, covering every theatre of war, and fighting against all three of our enemies, German, Italian and Japanese, one of only three RAF squadrons to do so.

At the outbreak we, as a country, were grateful for all we could receive, and considered ourselves fortunate to have some well endowed friends. One such was His Exalted Highness the Nizam of Hyderabad, a highly respected Indian prince, who felt honoured to be able to equip a squadron with eighteen Spitfires, at £5000 apiece forming the Hyderabad Squadron for the princely sum (pardon the pun) of £90,000. The squadron badge would portray his distinguished highness's hat and be inscribed with the motto 'Faithful Ally'.

Squadron commanders come and go, as do most flying personnel during the active life of a squadron, but ground crew, the backbone of a fighting team, usually remained throughout. I was fortunate enough to meet one of 152's most celebrated ground crew, one who had joined the squadron almost at its reincarnation, and although my own brother flew with the squadron from March 1943, I have no hesitation in dedicating this history to Sergeant Armourer Ray Johnson.

Through many fortuitous circumstances, notably the unique Black Cat, I met Ray a couple of years before his eightieth birthday, which incidentally I also attended, giving me the opportunity to meet a couple of other octogenarian ex-152 pilots whom I shall be delighted to name at a later stage as the saga of 152 unfolds. Our coming together took place at Duxford aerodrome during the Flying Legends air show of 1998, and from that meeting Ray very kindly lent me his audio tapes which he'd compiled from wartime memories.

This history is therefore a compilation derived from first-hand observation and participation by Ray Johnson and my brother Leonard Alfred Smith, together with such material and data that I have been both fortunate and grateful to have obtained through research.

Ray's war, as with all Johnsons, would be Johnny's war. Just as Len's war would be Smithy's war.

BRITAIN

1939–42

Slim and small in stature with rounded features and dark wavy hair, Ray wasted no time in enlisting, badgering the RAF in July 1939; and by the 12th with the number 650494 was marched off for his introduction to square bashing, plus the usual spit and polish associated with indoctrination into His Majesty's forces.

War was declared one day before his nineteenth birthday, being the 4th September, and it was soon after this at a temporary posting Ray tells us that with no knowledge of allied or enemy aircraft or of a Lewis gun, he was ordered to man the perimeter defence as part of everyone's protection. Fortunately, much to his relief, no attack materialised, and by the following 26th January with greater expertise under his belt caught up with the newly reformed No. 152 Squadron at RAF Acklington, quite close to the Northumberland coastline. Together they now formed part of Number 13 Group.

The aircraft dotted about the field were the soon-to-be-obsolete Gloster Gladiator biplanes; these relied on two Browning machine-guns fixed to the lower wings and two more synchronised with interrupter gear to fire through the propeller from in front of the pilot's cockpit. No. 152 became operational with these machines on 6th November, being tasked with convoy escort duties off the east coast.

At this juncture due to lack of aircraft, Ray informs us, sections of 152 suffered secondment to Sumburgh in the Shetland Isles, to grant greater range for convoy protection.

By early December little had happened in the way of action, with only friendly aircraft being sighted. Even so this gave them a good opportunity to exercise scramble procedures whilst intercepting these unidentified machines. Then their Spitfires began to arrive – Mk Is with the 1050 hp

Birth of the Black Panthers

Merlin engine and eight Browning machine-guns, four in each wing; their trajectory angled to miss the propeller and converge some 300 yards beyond, a distance that could be adjusted if the commanding officer so desired.

Maximum firing time was fourteen seconds.

On January the 6th 1940, the squadron became fully operational with these Spits, but unfortunately, that winter was such an atrocious one with extreme minus temperatures and heavy snow, that they were forced to revert to their trusty Gladiators. These machines were so much better able to cope with these types of conditions on a grass airfield.

Then on 3rd February their skipper, Squadron Leader Freddie Shute, flying a Gladiator, caught up with and shot down a Heinkel He 111. Again later that month he was scrambled over Farne Island, where another Heinkel bit the dust, but sadly Freddie failed to return, leaving his place to be taken by Squadron Leader Peter K Devitt.

Five months after the declaration of war, 152's (and Ray's) battle had been joined.

The whole squadron were badly cut up over the loss of Freddie, most ranks remembering him fondly and enviously because of his lovely sports car, the SS100 Jaguar, forerunner to the Jaguar XK120.

The last they'd seen of him was his Gladiator disappearing into a snow blizzard.

The Station Warrant Officer at this time was a chap called Tom. Ray says he was known as Tam Hill and was of such a senior age as to have probably been part of the RAF before Ray was born. Another character well remembered was the NCO in charge of B Flight ground crew, Chiefy Barnes. Apparently you could always tell the time of day by the angle of Barnes' forage cap. Starting off at KRs (King's Regulations) front above the right eye, and gradually as the day wore on for some obscure reason moving clockwise on his head, until come stand-down it would be practically at right angles.

The poor chap also suffered from a bad stutter, but with it displayed a great sense of humour, which was just as well, when one evening all hands as usual began heaving the Gladiators back into the hangars for the night. A large empty oil drum lay in their path which in the fading light became obscured, until Barnes uttered a staccato 'Mind that bloody dddrr— Oh tooooo pppiiiisssiiing late!!' Bods were beginning to fall about in uncontrollable laughter which as luck would have it also convulsed their Chiefy.

Another humorous story related tells of the purchase during this period of an old banger by three of the lads, a 1929 Swift for the princely sum of twenty pounds. This was fine until one of the erks decided to remove the brake shoes for repair, replacing all four wheels in the meantime. Unaware of this the other two took the car for a spin, travelling several miles without crashing before discovering the defect. One of these part owners survived the war and was residing in Weymouth in 1990.

By early April, No. 72 Squadron had arrived at Acklington, commanded by Sqn Ldr Ronnie Lees. The Spits could now be used but quite often the ground was so soggy that when taxying they were inclined to dig their wheels in and if not careful nose over, causing damage to the aircraft. To avoid this risk, an erk would prostrate himself across the tail, and when reaching position for take off, jettison himself, whilst at the same time giving a hefty bang to the side of the fuselage to warn the pilot he was clear.

On one occasion, one of the erks attached to 72 failed to eject himself quickly enough remaining sprawled precariously in front of the tail. But realising what must have happened as he suffered severe heaviness from the controls, the pilot continued to perform a perfect circuit, landing his plane and precious cargo without damage to either.

The incident made the national press, for which the Air Ministry were not amused when discovering details had been released through other than official channels.

In late May or early June a detachment of Spits was sent further south to Usworth in Co. Durham, just below Gateshead, and soon after this other orders arrived for all the Spits to make haste for Prestwick on the northwest coast near Ayr. A skeleton ground force was to join them by road, news having trickled through that the Germans were on the point of paying the areas around the Forth and Clyde a visit.

Ground staff were hastily billeted in tents and fed within the airport restaurant. Excellent food, remarked Ray, full of nostalgia, although to be fair also awarding brownie points for their stay at Acklington, especially recalling the 10:00 am NAAFI break with hot meat pies soaking up steaming mugs of char! Local pubs came in for critical acclaim at this point too. Such names as The Redrow, Broomhill, Amborth and Warkworth, allowing many grateful populace to ply our boys with northern hospitality.

Birth of the Black Panthers

However, having swept decisively across Europe, the Luftwaffe stood poised in northern France and the powers that be decided the time was now fast approaching to protect our southern shores. By July the 12th Ray found himself ensconced inside the narrow fuselage of a Handley Page Harrow, a high-wing twin-engine lumbering aircraft with fixed undercarriage that deposited him as part of an advance party at Warmwell, this being another pre-war grass airfield somewhere between the delights of Bournemouth and Weymouth and close to England's southern shore. Nearby lay the Army preserves of Bovington Camp, and historically just beyond the spot where our long lost hero Lawrence of Arabia met with a fatal motorcycle accident.

There was a concrete apron in front of the hangars which everyone was pleased about, but within a week their station commander, a Group Captain, holding court in front of the whole squadron, soon wiped the smiles off their faces.

'Ahem!' he said, taking time to clear his throat, 'One of these days in the not too distant future, the Hun is going to appear over those Purbeck hills,' he waved his arm in their general direction, 'and knock three different kinds of shit out of us! Therefore,' he continued, '152 Squadron is going to disperse to the far side of the airfield and hopefully ensure that little damage as possible is occasioned. The hangars,' he went on, 'will only be used for major inspections and repairs.'

Everybody's shoulders sagged a little, but the boss was right, before the battle was over Warmwell would be clobbered several times, but thankfully not quite so badly as those airfields further east.

Squadron duties were to be the defence of Portland Naval Base, Southampton Docks, Yeoville aircraft factories and the city of Bristol, to name but a few, and throughout the battle 152 would give a good account of itself. Considering that reports of enemy aircraft destroyed were often somewhat exaggerated, for whatever reason, the squadron still managed to receive final confirmation after the war of at least fifty to sixty victories over the enemy.

Days at dispersal soon became hectic, from dawn to dusk; always they seemed to be at readiness. This in truth was not always so, but with the ever increasing demands of rearming, refuelling, and constant daily inspections, duties seemed to follow each other without pause.

With the return of each aircraft ground staff would rush to greet their charges, thrilled at the sight of open gun ports and tell-tale black streaks on the underside of wings signifying that guns had been fired in combat. Quite often before lowering their undercarriage, pilots would perform victory rolls, causing everyone to jump up and down with excitement.

Sometimes an aircraft didn't return, then as all eyes and ears strained for the slightest sign, doubts would begin to creep in, with ground and aircrew alike becoming anxious for any news. Other Spits would land shot up, sometimes quite badly.

Flight Lieutenant Boitel-Gill pancaked in the corner of the field one day. Gill was a tall calm laconic type, totally unflappable, who always sported a long cigarette holder, carrying it with him wherever he went. Crews sped across the field to check on Gill, astounded as they surveyed the number of bullet holes in his machine, at least seventy entries being counted which had destroyed his undercarriage mechanism and flap controls.

As the inveterate smoker alighted from the wreck, calmly pressing a cigarette into its holder, he remarked to all and sundry, 'Thought I'd best put her in the corner of the field so she's tucked out of the way.' Then without a backward glance strolled off in the direction of the Ops room.

On another occasion Flying Officer Graham 'Cocky' Cox landed with his head and shoulders protruding beyond the top of his cockpit. Apparently his seat supports had collapsed either through enemy action or violent evasive action being taken, causing the seat to end up resting on his elevator and rudder controls.

Someone who had two very lucky escapes was a mountain of a man, namely Flying Officer Christopher 'Jumbo' Deansley, having to be rescued on each occasion after ditching into the Channel. Deansley was later to become a night fighter pilot, surviving the war, and fifty years on was still thriving in Edgebaston, Birmingham.

One day Jerry started to concentrate his attacks on the airfields and of course Warmwell did not escape. Ray remembers seeing about a dozen-plus aircraft approaching at eight to ten thousand feet and dropping their pretty accurate loads within minutes. Hangars and a number of aircraft were destroyed or damaged, plus a gaggle of unexploded bombs left littering the airfield These detonated themselves over the following few days. All in all a nasty day's work, causing many casualties amongst the ground crew.

Practically all ground crew working hours were now spent at the remote dispersal points near wooded areas at the far side of the field. As the future unfurled, 'to the woods!' became a clarion call whenever panic situations arose.

Towards the end of the long hot summer half a dozen of the lads were enjoying a well-earned break, this time given by the WVS. Types reckoned they were just that little bit more special than the normal NAAFI cuisine. Suddenly somebody spied a lone raider streaking towards the field at zero feet. It was a day of particularly poor visibility, and there was no time to run. Hardwood tables were standard issue in those days, and Ray remembers hurling himself beneath one just as the bombing and strafing took place, hearing an almighty thump as a large heating radiator torn from its mountings and catapulted across the room landed fairly and squarely on the table. Some, he reminisced, were definitely luckier than others.

A sad loss recalled during the battle was a twenty-one-year-old pilot by the name of Pilot Officer Douglas Shepley. He'd only been married six weeks, and had recently lost his Flight Lieutenant brother over Dunkirk. To make matters worse his sister, travelling overseas as a nurse, was lost when the SS Lancastrian was bombed and sunk. The family home was known as Woodthorpe Hall near Sheffield, and Dougie's wife Biddy, together with his parents, started a Spitfire fund, raising enough money to supply just such an aircraft to the RAF. To this day there is a pub near Woodthorpe Hall called the Shepley Spitfire.

On the 18th October 1940 the Daily Mirror newspaper carried a list of flying awards amongst which two were attributable to 152. Flight Lieutenant Derek Pierre Aumale Boitel-Gill DFC was approximately one month from his promotion to Squadron Leader and his taking command of 152 from Sqn Ldr Devitt. Boitel-Gill was considered a crack shot, having been credited with five kills in the month of August alone. (He was later to become a Wing Commander in June 1941, only to lose his life in a flying accident one month later in July.) The other was P/O Walter Beaumont DFC, unfortunately this officer being lost before he could receive the award. One other reference was a DFC to a certain Flt Lt J E J Sing, this gentleman by a strange twist would become 152's commander some two years hence when the squadron found itself about to embark overseas.

All squadrons had a mascot and 152 was no exception, almost from the outset a white bull terrier who answered (I use the term loosely) to the name of Pooch became theirs. Now Pooch was definitely not an easy animal to get along with, and if he only suspected you were scared of him it was sufficient to make your life a misery and invariably hazardous. A certain parachute packer was one such person. Among his various duties there entailed trips to the pilots' hut or tent, whichever it happened to be, to complete his daily inspections. Somehow Pooch always sensed his coming from afar, and it was left to whoever dared to grab hold of Pooch, to picket him down. A daunting task for Pooch had been known to move a NAAFI wagon given a length of rope and a little encouragement.

Even up to this stage Pooch's career had been somewhat colourful. In early 1939 he'd belonged to a Canadian officer pilot stationed at Digby, seconded to the RAF for some scheme or other. On his return to Canada, Pooch found himself also transferred, to Tommy Thomas. Now Tommy got married and as men do he gave Pooch to his wife as a wedding present. Well for some time after the poor lady remained scared stiff, but gradually her nerves strengthened, until she and Pooch became very good friends.

When 152 eventually reformed in October 1939, Tommy became commander of B Flight and remained so until about September 1940, by which time he'd won promotion to Squadron Leader and along with his dear lady became posted elsewhere. A little prior to this Pooch had been offloaded and taken over by the squadron, or more precisely, by F/O Cocky Cox, Cocky of course being proportionately equivalent in weight and strength to Pooch but luckily with an infinitely more docile disposition. Cocky and Pooch became great buddies, and wherever the squadron went, so did Pooch. Right up to late 1942 Pooch was king of 152, where at each station posting pilots would tear around to make certain he didn't go short of feminine company. So much so, that Ray swears he had more nooky than the rest of the squadron put together.

Warmwell had actually been taken over on the 6th July when 609 (West Riding) Squadron arrived under the command of Sqn Ldr Horace Stanley 'George' Darley. Attached to No. 10 Group, of which 152 would become a part, they had been given a scramble time of fifteen minutes.

As the battle began to unfold so the history of 152 Squadron pilots would be etched forever in the annals of the RAF, and their first casualty at Warmwell became P/O Frederick Hyam Posener, a twenty-three-year-old South African volunteer shot down in an attack off Swanage on the 20th July, only the second day of the squadron's active service from their new airfield.

The 25th saw revenge taken by the C/O, Sqn Ldr Peter Devitt, when he led 152 over Portland, getting a Dornier and some Junkers Ju 87 'Stuka' dive bombers, with Bob Wolton and Jumbo Deanesley.

On the 8th August two 152 pilots successfully escaped from crash landings after hectic dogfights, Sgt Denis Norman Robinson ending up with his fuselage standing vertically with its propeller embedded in a meadow, and P/O Walter Beaumont pancaking in a field. This officer made a double kill of two Messerschmitt Bf 109s on the 16th August, and on the 27th, after sharing in the honour of downing a Heinkell He 111, was forced to bail out over the sea, and survived yet again.

On the 15th a mass of enemy aircraft had been intercepted approaching Portland Naval Base. Numbers were put at 100-plus with nine Spits from 152 diving out of the sun. Sgt Denis Robinson shot down a Messerschmitt Bf 110, with Bob Wolton clambering from his cockpit seconds before his Spit hit the sea, and P/O Harold John Akroyd limping home with a jammed rudder.

On the day Denis Robinson claimed yet another victory over a Ju 88, Sgt John Barker was lost.

Sept. 15th dawned, the day later to become known as 'the end of the beginning'. One of 152's pilots up this day was P/O Eric Marrs. Marrs had become christened 'Boy' Marrs because although he was only nineteen years old he looked decidedly younger. His career to date had been meteoric, with kills already to his credit, and today would be no exception as leading B Flight he dived on a formation of thirty Heinkell He 111 bombers. The Spits harried them for ten miles and Marr's cursed that the whole squadron wasn't with them. They shot down two and damaged many others. Pilots involved in this action were P/O Peter O'Brien, Sgt Kenneth Holland, and P/O Watson.

Unfortunately, two days later, after shooting down a Ju 88 Marrs suffered an engine failure and had to coax his faithful Spit, which he had flown for 130 hours, down from 12,000 feet to a concrete runway on a disused and obstructed airfield at Yatesbury. Apparently a stray bullet had smashed his air cooler, causing the aircraft to go out of service, and she would never return to 152.[1]

On this day Hitler postponed indefinitely his planned invasion of Great Britain, called Operation Sea Lion. Despite this rethink, however, aerial

---

1 These actions have been corroborated from *Battle of Britain Dorset* by the late Rodney Legg.

battles would still go on.

On September 19th Sgt Holland sent a Ju 88 diving into the sea with both engines on fire, but on the 23rd P/O Beaumont was lost, believed shot down over the sea.

Sgt Holland again saw action on the 25th, bringing down a Heinkell 111, but sadly Holland himself crash landed, dying almost immediately, having suffered from a bullet to the head which had obviously contributed to the forced landing.

Boitel-Gill again led his section against Ju 88s escorted by Bf 109s west of the Isle of Wight on the 26th, where 'Bob' Wolton downed a Bf 109, but the squadron lost Sgt Jack Mcbean Christie, and it was during this action that 'Jumbo' Deansley once more bailed out over the sea.

The 27th saw 'Boy' Marrs have a running fight with a Ju 88, at times flying as low as fifty feet as they headed for Porlock, west of Minehead. The Ju 88 ended up in the sea about twenty feet from the beach, with Marrs circling and waving from overhead, watching hordes of civilians rushing headlong to capture the crew. 'I watched the crew taken prisoner beat up the beach and then climbed away,' Marrs said. On the 30th however, after Sqn Ldr Devitt was only able to muster eight Spits to stop an attack on Sherbourne, Marrs' plane suffered an undercarriage malfunction leaving one wheel permanently down for landing. Unable to do a normal wheels-up pancake Marrs was forced to bring her in gently as possible, with the plane ending up sliding sideways on one main wheel plus tailwheel and wingtip. 'I hopped out and went straight to the MO,' said Marrs, 'to get lots of metal splinters removed from my leg and wrist. Must say it felt good to be on terra firma.'

This same day saw the sad loss of twenty-six-year-old Sgt Leslie Arthur Edwin Reddington, who went into the sea still strapped in his Spit.

Not to be put off, Marrs was up once more on the 7th October, when bombers were reported headed for the Westland aircraft factory at Yeovil. Leading Blue Section at 20,000 feet he peeled off to attack a Bf 110, which soon showed signs of coolant loss as the glycol streamed from its starboard engine. Suddenly the complete rear section of its cockpit flew off and both crew members jumped out. Orbiting above, Marrs watched as the Messerschmitt dove into the sea and both parachutists were captured by the Army.

On 8th October P/O Harold John Akroyd, bringing his crippled Spit into a field near Nutmead, Shillingstone after a dogfight over west Dorset, unfortunately caught fire and although managing to escape the flames, later died from his burns. Aged twenty-seven years he was buried at Warmwell.

Another pilot from 152, Sgt Edmond Eric Shepperd, was killed on the 18th October, when for no apparent reason his plane suddenly plunged into the ground at Tadnol Mill two miles south-east of Warmwell Airfield.

It was reported in October that Pooch, who had supposedly sired most of the bull terriers in the RAF, had been given the honorary rank of Pilot Officer.

Eric 'Boy' Marrs was again making a name for himself on 14th November when with Sgt Albert Wallace 'Bill' Kearsey they were scrambled to intercept a Junkers Ju 88 heading for Yeovil. Attacking from beneath Marrs gave a burst from only 150 yards, causing an immediate fire in the port engine; at the same time however the German rear gunner splintered Marrs' windscreen, turning it opaque. Now unable to continue he was forced to become an observer watching Kearsey chasing the Ju 88 down from 24,000 feet to 5,000 feet. Kearsey by this time was out of ammo, but the German had become a fireball. A crewman was seen to bail out but his chute failed to open, and he fell through the roof of Kinson Potteries. With the remaining crew on board the Junkers continued on attempting to achieve straight and level flight, but at the last moment it struck the ground on the corner of Ringwood Road and Herbert Avenue, exploding on impact.[2]

Ray makes mention of two Polish pilots attached to 152, nicknamed Zig and Zag. Zig was lost on the 28th November and I can now record the action also corroborated by some details from the late Rodney Legg.

November had been a particularly quiet month overall, but this day Sgt Zygmunt Klein had been scrambled, along with P/O Arthur Ray Watson and 'Boy' Marrs, over the Needles at the Isle of Wight, where they immediately bumped into some Bf 109s and dogfights ensued.

Zig apparently just disappeared, while Watson was forced to bail out. Unfortunately he tore his parachute in the attempt, and fell with the canopy streaming out behind him.

Both pilots were instantly avenged when Marrs managed to unleash just a one-second burst towards one of the 109s. Astounded by the results

---

2 Once again the actions depicted from fifteenth of September have been endorsed by *Battle of Britain Dorset* as well as by Ray Johnson.

from such a small number of bullets, when black smoke poured from the German plane and oil spewed over his own windscreen.

He was forced to half roll and dive away, trying to follow the German in a steep spiral, as he watched flaming fragments breaking from it. Then one large lump broke away that was not on fire, trailing a white plume which turned into a parachute. The pilot had managed to bail out just before his fuel tank exploded. 'He landed in the sea,' said Marrs, 'but might just as well have stayed with the plane for he was never found.'

The following day P/O John Woodward Allen was scrambled to 25,000 feet over Warmwell with other members of the squadron when a German fighter sweep was suspected. He later sent an unintelligible radio message, before complete silence. His Spitfire was then seen to break away in a shallow dive, which gradually became vertical, ending up plummeting straight into a wood half a mile from the Travellers Rest, two miles from Durweston. Oxygen failure was the verdict given. The site was eventually marked in 1978 by a granite memorial.

By Christmas, Ray would enjoy a welcome spell of leave; he had missed the previous Christmas, and for the first time in a long while could journey to Grantham safe in the knowledge that England in all probability was now free from invasion. Upon his return the RAF thanked him kindly by bestowing upon him the exalted rank of Leading Aircraftman, giving him a pair of propeller chevrons to sew on his sleeves.

As days became shorter so air activity reduced correspondingly, with much more time off being allowed. This gave Ray and his ground buddies a chance to get around the neighbouring area. Visiting places such as Bournemouth and Weymouth, and whenever funds stretched to it all the local hostelries in nearby Woodsford, Puddletown, Broadmayne, and Dorchester. Pilots had their own favourites, one of which I visited in this year 2001 called The World's End, near Tolpuddle. A lovely low ceiling, log fired, thatched building signifying everything they had been fighting for.

Come February 1941 the pilots thought it about time to honour their ground crews, they knew above everything else just how important these guys were. Whenever they threw their leg over the side of the cockpit and settled down to be strapped in by their anxious helper, it meant they could concentrate on the job in hand without having to worry about the serviceability of the machine they were about to fly.

Birth of the Black Panthers

The Gloucester Hotel in Weymouth was everyone's favourite venue and 152 pilots plied their compatriots with appreciation straight from the bottle. Ray assures me it was an extremely heavy night.

The very next morning, their squadron commander, Sqn Ldr Boitel-Gill, whose favourite pastime was low flying, took off on a so-called air test with another Spit flown by Flt Lt Dennis David.

Having disappeared from view, they suddenly reappeared at zero feet, wingtip to wingtip, travelling at over 300 mph, each heading straight across the dispersal area. Ray recalls they were so low he actually noticed dirt and small stones sucked up by the wash of the propellers. After landing it was noted that Dennis David's airscrew in particular had score marks on each tip, which couldn't have done his engine any good either. In the meantime Dennis, so the story goes, had disappeared into the pilots dispersal hut for what everyone reckoned was a change of underwear.

Soon 152 would be on the move again, but I cannot leave this episode without some mention, despite the brave attempts by our pilots to avert the German onslaught, of the terrible suffering and dire consequences caused by those bombers that did get through.

The following paragraphs have been compiled from excerpts from Battle of Britain Dorset by the late Rodney Legg:

Before 609 squadron had arrived, Ju 87 Stuka dive-bombers were attacking shipping, the 4th July seeing one attack taking place at Portland Harbour itself. A dozen of the planes dived on the anti-aircraft auxiliary HMS Foylebank, where one of the first casualties was Leading Seaman Jack Mantle. Despite both legs being shattered in the attack, Jack stayed at his Pom Pom gun continuously firing as he received more fatal wounds. Fifty-nine others were killed and sixty injured. Jack Mantle was granted a posthumous V.C. for his courageous action.

But perhaps the unluckiest tale that day revolved around nine McAlpine workers who had been digging a tunnel. They had wisely sheltered inside their efforts until they thought the raid over, emerging to face a single bomber who had turned back from out at sea. The blast from its bomb killed them all, including four who were only boys.

By August attacks were becoming more concentrated on the

*actual coastline and on the eleventh more than 150 bombers and
fighters breached Weymouth and Portland. Fifty-eight bombs were
dropped in the borough, with many more falling into the sea. It was
a day of near misses and lucky escapes, only a main pipeline was
fractured with the loss of about 200 gallons of oil.*

*On the 21st two people were killed in Poole when a lone Ju 88
swept low over the old town area, and on the 23rd two more died at
Lulworth from a lone raider attack, with twenty-four people being
killed at New Milton after a Ju 88 devastated Station Road.*

*There were almost daily raids of course, with reports of bombs
and incendiary devices falling all over the place. Near Christchurch
Priory, Hoburne Farm, Chewton Common, on Iford golf course,
and many more at Poole and Portland.*

*Two hundred and twenty attacking planes dropped 350 bombs
from 15,000 feet onto the Bristol Aeroplane Company's works in
September, with Westland's Yeovil factory also being targeted the
same month. In this latter raid the town of Sherborne suffered a
spate of sixty bombs within a few minutes. Townsfolk felt afterwards
that casualties had been light considering the devastation wrought:
seventeen dead and thirty-two injured.*

These were just some of the happenings around Warmwell that swept into
history as Britain and 152 prepared for the next phase.

But before 152 left for pastures new, Ray has one last tale to tell, firstly
by reminding us about the sad demise of Zig, and how his compatriot Pole,
Zag, survived the war, and in 1990 actually lived in London. Finally Ray
went on to relate one of those many unfortunate and bizarre consequences of
war. Pilots were seated in the sergeants' mess just as, in the jargon of the day;
a nuisance raider came across the airfield. It was shooting its guns as it swept
in low, and a single bullet struck a fatal blow to Spitfire pilot Sgt Fawcett.

Lying further west in the county of Cornwall, Portreath became the
proud host to 152 on the 9th April 1941. Almost immediately they were
issued with what Ray calls an abomination, a Spitfire fitted with a thirty-
gallon overload tank permanently fixed to the underside of the port wing.
He had it on good authority that only two other squadrons were so adorned.
Take offs and landings would now require all the right rudder and trim that
one could muster.

Birth of the Black Panthers

From April to August duties would consist of convoy patrols, and escorts to our bombers attacking the German battleships Gneisenau and Scharnhorst, anchored in the port of Brest. Bombers used on these operations would be mainly Bristol Blenheims and Handley Page Hampdens.

Everyone now knew the reason for the extra fuel tank; their Spits would need it to cater for the greater range.

At this stage of the war, Brest without doubt was one of the most heavily defended areas in Europe. A fact fully confirmed by none other than Wing Commander Guy Gibson himself. Flak could be expected from a few hundred feet to several thousand in dense concentration.

Two pilots were to be lost during these holocaust operations: Sgt Short who became a prisoner of war, and Eric 'Boy' Marrs DFC, who sadly fell foul of the deadly ack ack that spewed from every direction. Germany paid great honour to this brilliant young man, giving him a full military funeral at Brest cemetery. Marrs had been awarded his DFC on 31st December 1940, and had been to the palace with another DFC winner, Dudley Williams, to receive it in March 1941. That last flight took place on the 24th July, just twenty days after his twentieth birthday. Everyone who knew him, all his comrades and crew, always swore he would never be shot down by any German fighter pilot. A prophecy that was proved correct.

Food at Portreath, at least as far as other ranks were concerned, was about the worst that Ray had encountered. The station itself was incomplete and if one were making excuses maybe this could be the reason. In any event types found themselves at various opportunities, having to augment their rations by consuming large quantities of egg on toast from the café just rear of the beach at Portreath, and another establishment quite close to their domestic quarters, being at the bottom of a steep track and across a road. Here the landlord's wife for the chosen few would make excellent Cornish pasties. Some twenty-five years later, Ray returned to find the same landlord still in residence, but sadly his wife had passed away a few years earlier.

The airfield, indeed the whole camp, was actually perched on a rocky headland about 200 feet above sea level, and mists, or frets as they were sometimes called, could spring up at this time of year quite quickly, and be of considerable density. On these occasions, landings, especially with long-range fuel tanks fitted, could be doubly difficult. A tragic victim of these conditions was P/O Rowlands. It is believed he allowed his speed to drop off as he made his curved approach, this being the standard configuration for a Spit. He hit the headland hard, being instantly killed in the ensuing inferno.

Another pilot of similar rank to Rowlands, P/O Mike 'Pop' Gardener was assigned to accompany the coffin from the Station to Bristol, arriving at 4:00 am, to be met by Mr Rowlands senior, Mike having the onerous task of consoling the family.

With 152's C/O he arranged for a flight of aircraft to perform a fly-past salute at Canford cemetery, expecting at least a couple of Spits from the squadron. In the event a flight of Westland Whirlwinds from 263 Squadron did the honours. Mike recalled that he didn't think anyone noticed that they weren't Spitfires, and although the Whirlwind pilots would not have known Ron Rowlands, they did enjoy the low flying between the barrage balloons. In fact the write-up in the local press made much of it, saying his comrades from his squadron flew past in salute.

Mike Gardener, continuing his recollection, did say that the squadron intelligence officer, Leslie Hiscock, had briefed him quite forcefully on the procedures for retrieving the ensign that draped the coffin. 'Watch the undertaker like a hawk,' he said.

Another armourer, by the name of Charlie Colman, sometimes stayed out overnight with Ray at Penzance, one of their favourite haunts being the Yacht Inn near the swimming pool. In the early hours of the morning they would sneak back into camp aboard the civilian works bus which entered unnoticed through a rear entrance leading from the harbour.

Such indiscipline was unknowingly rewarded when Ray suddenly found himself the proud recipient on the 15th August of corporal stripes, duly placed in charge of A Flight armourers, and granted seven days' leave to saviour the prospect.

Like all good sons, Ray thought it was about time to take mum a nice load of washing, somehow service life never catered for laundry care especially when you were in home waters, so without further ado Ray cadged a spare parachute bag from his Pooch-pestered friend. All was fine until reaching his final destination, Grantham railway station.

Approached by two officious looking military police, Ray never batted an eye when asked to disclose what goodies he held in the bag. After all, he'd just come all the way up country including the nightmare journey across London, without so much as a sideways glance. 'Dirty washing,' threw Ray, already turning towards the station entrance and home. Patience was not a commodity after so much strain.

'Oh! Let's see,' said one of the types, 'open up the bag!'

Ray was peeved, to say the least, his arrival had coincidentally seen the station clock reach 4:00 am. 'I refuse,' he puffed, 'unless its in the presence of an officer.' That'll show 'em, he thought.

Not to be outdone, they marched Ray back to the station innards where they brought the RTO[3] from his pit. Carefully he listened to Ray's explanations, and then as though to appease his accusers, he suggested Ray empty his bag anyway.

'Fair enough,' croaked Ray, 'there you are,' straight away emptying the entire contents over the RTO's desk. Ray said afterwards that his feet weren't so well behaved in those days either, which definitely did not improve matters.

The final outcome to all this was that Ray found himself in front of his commanding officer, charged with being in unauthorised possession of a parachute carrying bag. The poor parachute packer who had stuck his neck out for Ray received a rollicking, but when Ray explained his story the C/O laughed like a drain and told his corporal to get lost.

The commanding officer issuing this judgement was Squadron Leader Jackie Darwen. This officer had taken command from Boitel-Gill in June, on the latter's promotion to Wing Commander and subsequent posting to an Operational Training Unit.

Ray is able to fill us in on one or two more details concerning Boitel-Gill, whom we know was unfortunately killed in July. He was a very cool, calculating officer, Ray said, one with great flying experience, joining the RAF in 1929, to be followed by a period of flying attached to Imperial Airways, and finishing up prior to the outbreak of hostilities as none other than the Chief Pilot to his Highness the Nizam of Hyderabad.

'I understand,' said Ray, 'that it was while participating in some low flying in a Hawker Hurricane to give ack ack crews in the area a spot of practice, that his plane hit the deck.'

Jackie Darwen of course was also an excellent pilot, but with almost an opposite temperament. Ray tells us that the possible cause of this could

---

3 Railway Transport Officer. Ray states that these gentlemen were army officers and usually stationed at main line junctions of which Grantham was one.

have been due to a terrible tragedy that befell his C/O sometime before joining 152. Holding his wife in his arms as they danced at the Café-de-Paris in London, Jackie held tight when the room suddenly erupted. Two bombs dropped at the height of the Blitz had penetrated the hotel lift shaft, instantly wiping out Ken 'Snakehips' Johnson and his band, along with many others, including poor Jackie's wife, still clutched to his chest.

The sad episode poignantly highlighted by the portentous words of her father still ringing in his ears as Jackie and his nineteen-year-old bride sailed from Rhodesia to fight for Great Britain: 'Take care of her young man,' he had emphasised. 'Remember you are taking my daughter into a war zone.'

Ever since that day Sqn Ldr Darwen never seemed to bother about his own life. When he left the squadron with promotion in March 1942, he became posted to the Desert Air Force in the Western Desert, and flew cover for the Eighth Army. Eventually he commanded a crack Hurricane squadron, with a skeleton ground crew that operated behind enemy lines, causing great disruption and havoc to German lines of communication. They used to hide the aircraft in redoubts dug several feet into the sand then cover them with camouflage netting. This type of operation, Ray reckons, would have suited Jackie down to the ground. The only other bit of information Ray has is that his old commander did get killed sometime in 1943.

For one week towards the end of August 1941, 152 would move to Snailwell, near Newmarket – presumably, so the rumour goes, to permit others to take over Portreath to continue hammering away at Hitler's two battleships still holed up in Brest. These ships, should they escape, could be a menace to all and sundry.

In any event, after Snailwell the squadron transferred to Swanton Morley until December, and then further east to Coltishall.

Still with the Mk II long range Spits, squadron duties would be confined to further convoy patrols, coupled with daylight escort duty to Blenheims attacking anything worthwhile along the Dutch coast. During this period explicit instructions were issued to pilots that under no circumstances should they be wooed by German fighters away from the Blenheims.

In essence one of their biggest headaches at this time was unfortunately our own Navy. I have it on good authority from my own brother that they would quite often mistake our aircraft for the enemy. All the more frustrating when one thinks of the distinctive silhouette of a Spitfire. Ray confirms that in spite of showing the colours of the day, naval ships patrolling the convoys shot two of 152's Spits out of the sky. Sgt Axe, a Canadian, was one, lost just off Cromer.

A bit of good news was that Sgt 'Taxi' Marsh accounted for a Bf 109 whilst stationed at Swanton Morley.

Vernon Shaw, an armourer friend of Ray's who had joined 152 at a similar period, cornered his colleague one day to impart some dreadful news. He'd just received an urgent telephone call informing him that both his parents and sister had been killed during a blitz on Merseyside. His home had received a direct hit. Ray recalls the distraught Vernon later married a WAAF from Abergavenny.

The last week in the year fell due whilst the squadron still operated from Coltishall. The festive season would be split, with half the lads celebrating Xmas at home, and the other half bringing in the New Year with their loved ones.

In those days, Grantham was a railway crossroads; whether you travelled east, west, south or north, you could bet your life at some stage you would find yourself disgorged onto Ray's home platform. Having to struggle with kit bags, rifles, tin hats and the lot, and usually at some ungodly hour to await belching, grinding steam-horses to carry you further to your destination. Ray's luck of the draw fell into the second category, along with three or four Scots and Geordies. After a long and tedious roundabout journey, they were thankful when Ray suggested, why didn't they all kill time by coming home with him for some home-cooked refreshment.

It was a typical gesture in those days to have your favourite son turn up out of the blue with half his buddies at an hour when everyone was safely tucked up in bed. Ray's parents took matters in their stride, but afterwards his dad confided that he couldn't understand a word all his foreign friends were talking. 'God I thought for one horrible moment you'd joined the Luftwaffe,' he joked.

Other reminiscences of Ray's, which in truth many people would find uneventful, and perhaps uninteresting, nevertheless help to convey what after all is part of wartime life when attached to an RAF squadron. He tells of visiting the local area around Coltishall, drinking in the Adam and Eve pub at a village called Little Hautbois, unfortunately when looked for twenty years after the war, it was no longer there. Maybe demolished when

Coltishall's runway needed to be lengthened.

Once while sitting in the Castle Hotel, another favourite haunt, this time in Norwich itself, Ray couldn't resist asking for the umpteenth time of a colleague, why it was that just before he went home on leave he always put on the back of the envelope being posted to his wife, the word 'Norwich'. For some time past now Ray had noticed this and each time his enquiry had met with nondescript comment. This time Ray was determined to pin down this reluctance. 'Well if you must know,' said his recalcitrant comrade, 'it's a code which stands for "'nickers off ready for when I come home".'

A midwinter move across the Irish Sea is definitely not everyone's cup of tea, or glass of Guinness come to that. Fine for pilots swanning happily above, but that mid-January crossing to reach Eglinton near Londonderry during a snowstorm was not one to endear itself to hard working ground crews. From Fleetwood to Belfast was one journey too far for some. Ray recalls that his parachute packing friend, currently under close arrest for some obscure offence, could be seen wandering aimlessly about the deck searching vainly for his escort who unbeknown to him were busily spewing up their insides, neither could care less what their errant captive got up to.

Only a single thought controlled the minds of all: 'What a way to run a bloody war.'

For the next six months Eglinton would be their new home, tasked with convoy patrols interspersed with air gunnery exercises, both air to air and air to ground, still with their long range Mark II Spits – abortions, which many felt were the cause of constant fatal accidents suffered by 152. Two more experienced pilots would crash unexpectedly, Flt Lt Bogle Bodie DFC and Flt Lt Southill. Bogle was a Battle of Britain ace and a most excellent fellow. Such a demise felt totally unnecessary and very sad: when carrying out aerobatics in front of the whole squadron, Bogle's plane for no apparent reason suddenly spun in.

By March it was Sqn Ldr Jackie Darwen's turn to be posted, and into his place stepped Sqn Ldr Harold Bird 'Birdie' Wilson. Here stood another very popular figure and excellent pilot drawn from the Battle of Britain. Birdie would survive the war, and for a number of years after continue to serve until reaching the high rank of Air Vice Marshal, acquiring in the process the OBE, DSO, DFC & bar, AFC & bar.

It soon became obvious to Birdie that 152 was in danger of becoming a supply squadron. In other words, training pilots for the mainland who were going on the offensive in more and more numbers as the war progressed. This format didn't suit Birdie and before long it became common knowledge that he was making quite a nuisance of himself trying to get the squadron moved to a bit of action.

About the middle of their stay at Eglinton in April '42, a unit of US Army Air Force personnel arrived, minus aircraft. A large number of brand-new Spits were assigned to them, which much to Ray's and others' disgust they proceeded to prang all over the airfield by the dozen. Seventeen in fact in one day alone, all the more galling because the Spits were so much better than 152's current complement.

During their time at Eglinton, a couple of opportunities arose for journeys home for Ray. This time it entailed catching the ferry from Larne to Stranraer, then rail to Sheffield, changing again at Wretford, and finally crawling home at an ungodly hour. I hope his parents appreciated it. As Ray is at pains to point out, one must remember that these wartime train journeys were a congested chaos, acquiring a seat was like winning a football pool, and even standing room in the corridors was at a premium.

Prior to their move to Eglinton F/O Cocky Cox left the squadron, taking Pooch with him, this meant 152 was suddenly bereft of a mascot. This slot was soon filled however when some of Ray's cronies purloined a young nanny goat, duly christened Bella.

In August instructions were received for the squadron to make for Gravesend. This order was almost immediately rescinded. Shortly after however fresh memos were forthcoming sending 152 to Angle, perched on the extreme southwest tip of Wales. Their stay would be short-lived, a mere four weeks, and although it was unknown at the time the beginning of Birdie's successful agitation, and the countdown to the squadron's overseas service.

During their stay at Angle, Birdie flew home in his Spit, to grab a spot of leave. When he came to complete the return however he was suddenly taken ill in the cockpit, and rushed to hospital with appendicitis. This was the call for Sqn Ldr Jackie Sing DFC to take command of 152.

Just down the road from Angle was Milford Haven, and the Short Sunderland flying boat station: coupled with this, 152's junior NCOs had been issued with bicycles, liking nothing better than to utilise their new mode of transport to visit the local pub situated in a nearby cove. As luck would have it one of the corporals attached to the flying boat station also had a small motorised boat, this he was required to use each night to visit Lundy Island. Ray's memory is a little hazy now, and he swears it certainly was at the time, particularly the following morning, when trying to recall what the hell happened after leaving the pub and stumbling straight into the boat for an unscheduled trip on the high seas.

Wittering, near Stamford, was their next home, aircraft and personnel arriving on the 30th September 1942, where all clothing possessions were taken from them and new khaki battledress issued. Flashes, insignia, and badges of rank would still be in blue. They knew now that this would be their last station in the UK – for how long was anybody's guess, but as Ray said, for some flying personnel and ground crew it would definitely be their last.

Group Captain Basil Embry was the station commander at Wittering, and you could tell he didn't like his station being used for what he clearly saw as a transit camp.

With every day that passed gradually the squadron was being turned into a fully mobile and completely self-contained unit, with its own MT, admin and stores sections. This gave it a total strength of about 350 ground crew. All were now issued with small arms, including Sten guns and rifles. Senior NCOs would receive revolvers and commando knives, which worried everyone a little, and were given a course of instruction on there use. Where, they wondered, were they going, and more to the point, what did they expect them to do when they got there?

To avoid the station Groupie, whom they suspected was tearing his hair out, meant that most days were taken up with route marches, yet somehow those in charge always managed to rest the squads in Stamford about midday for an hour, just as the pubs opened.

Grantham at least now resided no more than twenty-five miles distant, so for the first time Ray could actually cadge a lift home quite readily whenever the opportunity prevailed. The only difficulty now was trying to explain to all and sundry why the hell he wore khaki instead of blue. Certainly when cornered by his old headmaster he took some convincing. Khaki after all was the colour of the RAF Regiment, and there was no way you could look after Spitfires if that was your unit.

Then one dark night towards the end of October or early November everyone found themselves herded on to Stamford Midland Station and squeezed into one long train. The powers that be never told you anything, surprise during the war was the essence of life. When daylight came all they could see was distant snow-covered mountains, actually they'd arrived at Greenock on the Firth of Clyde, not far from Port Glasgow, and the mountains ran down the side of Loch Lomond. Not that anyone had time to enjoy the view as they were ushered aboard the exalted SS Nea Hellas troopship. 'More like Near Hell,' said Ray.

Destined for they knew not where but fearing the worst.

Peering over the side Ray couldn't help reminiscing that his three years in Blighty had come to an end, little did he know then that the next three would be spent careering round the world fighting the Bosch, Italians and Japanese.

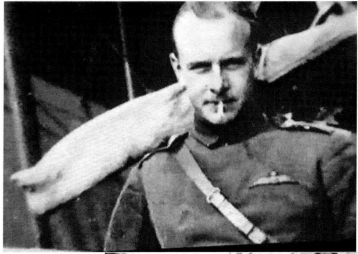

Top: 1918. Charles Chabot with Sopwith Camel
Middle: 1980. Charles Chabot alongside Bleriot
Above: 1980. Charles Chabot in cockpit of Bleriot

Middle of August 1940, 152 Squadron pilots and groundcrew (back row) at RAF Warmwell, with one of their Spitfires behind.

Front row (left to right):
1. Sergeant Pilot Jack McBean Christie (would be killed in action, 26 September 1940)
2. Pilot Officer Timothy Seddon Wildblood (missing in action, 25 August 1940)
3. The Squadron's Adjutant
4. Flying Officer Peter Geoffrey St George O'Brian (survived the war, becoming Group Captain in 1956 and ADC to the Queen in 1958)
5. Fkight-Lieutenant Derek Pierre Aumale Boitel-Gill (killed in flying accident, 18 September 1941)
6. Squadron Leader Peter Devitt (survived the war and into the 1990s, having retired as Wing Commander in 1945)
7. Flight-Lieutenant Frederick Mytton Thomas (survived the war, leaving as Wing Commander in 1945, and died in 1986)
9. The Squadron's Eingeer Officer
10. Pilot Officer Graham James Cox (survived the war, being released from the RAF was Squadron Leader, in 1946)
11. Sergeant Pilot Kenneth Christopher Holland (killed in action, 25 September 1940)

Middle row (left to right):
1. Sergeant Pilot Harold John Akroyd (fatally wounded in action 7 October 1940, dying the following day)
2. Sergeant Pilot Edmund Eric Shepperd (killed in flying accident, 18 October 1940)
3. Pilot Officer Richard Malzard Hogg (missing in action, 25 August 1940)
4. The squadron's Intelligence Officer
5. Pilot Officer Ian Norman Bayles (survived the war, being released from the RAF as Wing Commander, 1946)
6. Pilot Officer A. Weston (otherwise untraced)
7. Pilot Officer Walter Beaumont (missing in action, 23 September 1940)
8. Pilot Officer Charles Warren (survived the war, retiring from the RAF as Squadron Leader, 1957)
9. Pilot Officer Eric Simcox Marrs (killed in action, 24 July 1941)
10. Pilot Officer Frederick Henry Holmes (killed in action, 4 December 1944)
11. Sergeant Pilot John Keeth Barker (killed in action, 4 September 1940)
12. Sergeant Pilot Leslie Arthur Edwin Reddington (missing in action, 30 September 1940)

Centre:
Pilot Officer Pooch, mascot of 152 Squadron, who was said to have sired most of the bull-terriers in the Royal Air Force. Photo from Battle of Britain, Dorset.

1940. Sgt pilot Edmund Shepherd with Pooch

September 1940, Sergeant Pilot Edmund Shepperd with Pilot Officer Pooch, mascot of 152 Squadron, at RAF Warmwell. Shepperd, who was born at Binstead in the Isle of Wight in 1917, would be killed on 18 October 1940 when Spitfire R6607 crashed at Tadnoll Mill, between the aerodrome and Winfrith Heath.

1940. Warmwell – Sgt. Dennis Norman Robinson spitfire from 152 sqdn.

Sergeant Dennis Norman Robinson clambered from this cockpit after his 152 Squadron Spitfire plunged into meadows east of Wareham. Note the Squadron letters 'UM'.

1940. Sgt. Dennis Robinson

1940. Acklington
Ken Reeves with Ray Johnson on his left side

1940. Acklington
Ground-crew with Gladiator in background

Autumn 1940, four Spitfire pilots of 152 Squadron at RAF Warmwell: Flight Lieutenant Derek Boitel-Gill (left) commands 'A' Flight; Sergeant Pilots Howard Marsh (bottom left) and Jimmy Short are seen beside the dispersal hut, waiting the order to scramble; Sergeant Pilot 'Johnny' Johnston (below) is with his Mark I marchine.

1940. Warmwell
Flt/Lt Derek Boitel-Gill commander A Flight on left,

With Sgt. Pilots Howard Marsh and Jimmy Short bottom left and Sgt. Pilot Johnny Johnston leaning on 152 mark 1 spitfire.

1940. Warmwell
Zig Klein Polish pilot of 152

1940. Warmwell
Flt/Lt Boy Marrs DFC in cockpit of Old Faithful

1940. Warmwell
Flt/Lt Marrs DFC

ROYAL AIR FORCE STATION
WARMWELL
FORMERLY WOODSFORD
1937 – 1946
A MEMORIAL DEDICATED
TO THOSE MEN AND WOMEN WHO
WHILST SERVING WITH THE ROYAL
AIR FORCE, UNITED STATES ARMY
AIR FORCE, MILITARY AND ALLIED
FORCES AT R.A.F. WARMWELL
MADE THE SUPREME SACRIFICE
IN DEFENCE OF FREEDOM.
LEST WE FORGET. 11th JUNE 1988

2001 - Warmwell Memorial
Erected to all those who flew from Warmwell

TUNISIA–SICILY–ITALY

1942–43

For the time being, only the food and the weather would occupy everyone's mind. Both, it would appear, were appalling. Headed for who-knew-where as the seas became mountainous, every time the ship hit the crest of a wave her propellers sent grouching shudders through her superstructure.

Snow and ice were also a feature of everyday life.

As one of the more fortunate ones, Ray never suffered from sea or air sickness, but out of his mess table of fourteen souls, only two or three would deign to appear. A scenario that continued for several days. 'Those few that were fit,' he said, both eyes glinting, 'ignored the quality and scoffed the lot.'

Sleeping in hammocks they learnt the answer to two oft-spoken factors: the call, 'Wakey wakey, rise and shine, mash up and stow'; and why hammocks were not recommended for honeymooners.

Although they ate it, Ray couldn't help describing the food as peas dished up almost continuously that were akin to bullets and bread so infested with weevils that they reckoned they had fresh meat with their doorstop everyday.

He's unsure how or where they learnt of their destination, but he does remember passing through the Straits of Gibraltar at night and seeing the lights of Tangiers on their starboard beam, then finally disembarking at Algiers and getting away from the dockside pretty pronto.

Their first two nights were spent in bivouacs about a mile along the beach from dockland. Facing them across a stretch of road stood a French army barracks with colonial troops on guard. Ray shared his bivvy with his birthday twin, the parachute packer Roger Burns. They were two types who would share everything, their last cigarette, even their last two bob.

When morning came they were told to wash and shave in the sea, and given sea soap for the exercise. 'Awful,' said Ray, 'all it did was leave a horrible scum on your face and hands.' One thing about Burns was he always had a sharp wit, seeing the funny side of most things, but when Ray studied his compatriot this morning, his face remained stony and silent.

So much for their introduction to foreign lands.

On the third day they were told to gather up their kit, holdalls, kitbags, rifles etc. and marched smartly off about twelve miles to an airfield at Maison Blanche. During this period, unknown to them, their flying fraternity, shipped separately along with crated Mk VB Spitfires, had disembarked at Gibraltar. Here they would wait while their new Spits were built, serviced, fuelled and armed by a brand new type of personnel specifically trained as Servicing Commandos for just such a task.

These Spits now carried four .303 Browning machine-guns, and two 20 mm cannon; also like others of the Desert Air Force they were fitted with extra-large air filters over the air intake just below the propeller. This latter did effect the performance somewhat and consequentially deprived them of a few advantages previously held over the German 109s and Focke-Wulf 190s.

No. 152's pilots would fly their new machines to the port of Bone, on the coast near Bizerta, becoming immediately operational, carrying out patrols and offensive sweeps. From Bone the pilots eventually flew their Spits to Souk-el-Arba, an airstrip some seventy miles southwest of Tunis, where finally their ground crews caught up with them.

Ground staff could tell straight away that their pilots had certainly had a rough time of it since their arrival in North Africa. Sleeping, washing and shaving had been at a premium. Their C/O, Jackie Sing, and Flt Lt Sizer, one of their flight commanders, were both immediately taken ill and forced to spend some time in the field hospital. Ray remembered particularly how poorly his C/O looked with a substantial weight loss.

There had also been some casualties, with a number of new faces now in evidence. Crashing into the sea between Gibraltar and Algiers, Flt Lt Bassett had been their first loss.

But everyone was pleased to finally meet up with and greet each other, giving hearty handshakes and slaps across the back. Truly this was what exemplified squadron service, Ray never could get over the fantastic comradeship experienced.

Most squadron personnel would be known only by their surname, so when Ray joined he would be acknowledged as Aircraftman Johnson. As time progressed however and one became well known, Johnson would be replaced by Johnny, and as your service progressed higher ranks would also tend to address you in this more compatriot term. Certainly the pilot of your particular aircraft would, and as you achieved greater rank and responsibility, so your standing in the squadron would grow. When meeting pilots within the last few years that flew with my brother, they were totally surprised to learn that his Christian name was Len, only ever knowing and calling him Smithy.

Corporal Wiggly – now there's a name to conjure with – became 152's first overseas ground crew casualty. Ray uses the word loosely, for Wiggly, believe it or not, had to return to base hospital for none other than an urgent operation for circumcision. Can you imagine following his return to camp, the conversation piece for the next few weeks? 'Hi Wiggly!' they'd call, 'how's Fagin today?' To which he would reply, 'Fagin is very poorly,' and retrieve the doleful fellow for an airing complete with bandage and neatly tied bow.

Its easy for us today, in this western world of plenty, to forget how simple items of food used to concentrate the minds of fighting men so much in those austere times. Yet even so most were remarkably fit on it, which must surely announce something to our so often over-bloated bodies. Ray implies rations were monstrous, tinned Maconnickies " I guess type of Irish mutton stew" one day, and tinned corned beef the next. Corned beef done every which way you could think of: straight, battered, hashed, you name it, they had it!!

On occasion RAF cuisine was augmented with American K-rations, this contained powdered soup and chocolate amongst other things, it was enough for an emergency, which Ray's stomach always seemed to be suffering from.

They also had a free issue of cigarettes mixed in with their UK brands, which they would have to buy. The freebies were called C to C, which actually stood for 'Cape to Cairo'. Ray says, 'Pardon the expression, but they were crap, and known to all as "Camel to Consumer".' They used to barter them for eggs from the local Arabs. That is until even they wised up and refused all but British brands.

There was another free issue called Victory V, but the choice was immaterial.

Weather up to and including March 1943 had been the rainy season, leaving everything and everybody from their arrival until the end of that month with mud up to their eyeballs. Xmas and all things festive had just about been the most miserable time that anyone could ever remember.

You may recall the mention near the beginning of the lucky erk caught astride the rear end of a Spit at Acklington, 152's first stop after reforming. Well lo and behold if the damn thing didn't happen again at Souk-el-Arba, and this time Ray actually witnessed it and had the frantic task of informing Operations due to all other aircraft being currently airborne. This aircraft wasn't actually attached to 152 (or 72 which was the squadron associated with the previous episode) but the officer commanding the wing was none other than Ronnie Lees, now a Group Captain, who had been the Squadron Leader in charge of 72 when it happened at Acklington. This time however was not to be so fortunate, for the pilot, under advice or otherwise, approached for a wheels-up landing. The resulting impact catapulted the chap violently forward, causing him to finish up suffering two broken legs.

One day a formation of American bombers passed overhead at about seven to eight thousand feet, with everyone peering up thinking some poor bastard was going to get a packet full. 'They were certainly right,' said Ray, 'the idiots dropped the whole damn lot on Souk-el-Arba, it was only by a miracle they didn't clobber the airstrip.'

Most times, weather permitting, during the early months of '43, the odd enemy aircraft would come sweeping down the valley from the general direction of Tunis, shooting up and strafing anything that took their eye, such as road transport, Souk-el-Arba itself, and the airstrip in particular.

With 152's Spits on a sortie, most of the ground crew decided to enjoy a respite of chow and get cleaned up down in the village, where the station's cookhouse resided alongside their sleeping quarters in the Town Hall. Ensconced with the small party left holding the fort, Ray thankfully removed his tunic to bask in the afternoon sun, resting his limbs against the bell tent that served as the squadron's Ops room.

It was about 4:00 pm and before long a couple of 109s appeared overhead, types gave them a cursory glance but fortunately they seemed to be keeping well away. Then quite by chance Ray spotted a dot in the distance towards the south-west, watching fascinated as it curved towards the earth, gradually getting bigger and bigger, almost mesmerised as it grew into a Focke-Wulf 190.

One of the reserve pilots dashed from the tent, making for a nearby Spit, yelling for assistance. All Ray had time to see was the Spit erupt in a pall of smoke as he dived to the ground. He remembers vividly seeing these twinkling bright lights of the guns on the 190's wings, pointing straight at him. Nothing, he said, would ever erode that memory of those twinkling lights. Then the German was gone, screaming overhead and away. Bending to retrieve his battledress, Ray shivered when he saw the tattered remnants several bullets had passed through, leaving the waist belt hanging by threads.

The tunic became a symbol of good luck, tucked into the bottom of his kit bag wherever he went, until that is, almost at the war's end it mysteriously disappeared.

Pilots were on the move again, travelling to Souk-el-Khemis, before being directed to a place called Constantine. Here they would collect Spitfire Mk VBs adapted to carry two 250 lb bombs, one slung beneath each wing.

The bulk of the ground crew would be sent further back to the town of Setif for rest and recuperation before rejoining the squadron. Ray found himself, along with a few others, remaining at Souk-el-Arba.

The wheels of fortune move in mysterious ways, one moment thrown into the paths of danger whilst his comrades washed and ate, this time Ray was saved from possible bloody mishap by being left behind. Travelling through Setif in one of the station's wagons, twenty to thirty lads were struck side on by a hurtling locomotive as it passed through a level crossing. The number of dead escapes Ray's recollection now, but he can count Warrant Officer Barlow and Johnny Wilson among them.

The whole squadron were really shaken by this tragedy for quite a while, but one who did make a miraculous recovery despite appalling injuries was Jack Joseph. This gentleman was eventually discharged as an invalid, and was still going strong at Southsea as recently as 1993.

When the pilots did return with their adapted Spits to the forward area, the whole squadron decamped and moved further up the valley nearer Tunis to Souk-el-Khemis, where several all-weather strips had been prepared. The one occupied by 152 had a railway line running between the strip and their domestic quarters, where two or three times a week a train would arrive loaded with petrol in four-gallon cans, bombs and ammunition.

These they had to unload during the night, sending a call for all hands to the pumps, for the last thing anybody wanted was to be caught by Jerry with their pants down in this situation. A very fiddly and time-consuming task was having to fill the Spits from the four-gallon cans through chamois leather filters.

My brother, Leonard Alfred Smith, known in the squadron as 'Smithy', was born on 14th April 1920 and had left school at the age of fourteen: with such a lack of education, if he was ever going to fly a Spitfire he would have to do a Chabot. Air experience would surely make the difference, so in 1938 he joined the Civil Air Guard, soloing on a Gipsy Moth after five and half hours' practice, a school record at the time – somewhat different to Chabot's fifty minutes, but certainly in a more sophisticated aeroplane.

Before he reached Souk-el-Khemis he had what can only be described as a chequered career, for on November 27th 1941 he had deliberately flown his training Spitfire low over a lido at Littlehampton in which our widowed father, a tall silver-haired First World War veteran, worked. It was a building utilised to cater for evacuated children from the London bombings, and Dad, attached to the Greater London Council, helped look after them, being affectionately known by all the kids as Pop. The RAF found out about the incident because, unbeknown to my brother at the time, the topmost part of a flagpole standing high on the building had synchronised through his propeller and embedded itself in the root of his port wing. A further eight feet of the mast broke off and crashed through a glass dome attached to the roof.

Six months' grounding, three months' loss of sergeant's stripes and two weeks in His Majesty's Detention Barracks at Chatham would be Smithy's reward.

In RAF terms, such a disaster against one's character was denoted as a 'Black', and this was a very Big Black indeed. Recovery from this type of behaviour would be long and arduous, if at all. Only an exemplary service record from this moment could justify any advancement.

He eventually flew with 165 Squadron from Gravesend and later Tangmere, completing sweeps over France and bomber escort duties, and by February '43 was on the high seas sailing to catch up with Operation Torch.

Meeting up with 152 did not pose a straightforward exercise, in hindsight obviously due to their comings and goings at this particular moment. Smithy records being sent first to Setif, then Constantine, and then Souk-el-Arba, where on each occasion he missed 152 by a whisker. When he did eventually make contact at Souk-el-Khemis it was to arrive in what Ray called a sea of mud. This Smithy too relates vividly; that and crawling into a tent occupied by four other types, unknown to him, while at the same time nursing one terrible stomach ache.

By all accounts Len had reached Souk-el-Khemis just a little ahead of the newly adapted Spits, as arriving on the 14th March, it is not until his diary entry of the 18th does he complain that he's just heard they are changing onto Spit bombers. Still suffering from stomach pains on the 15th, he now finds there is no water to wash or shave with, and the mud is so bad vehicles are constantly getting bogged down including the C/O's wagon.

The following day he managed to get airborne. 'Stooging around getting acquainted with the terrain, waiting to get jumped' is the way he described it. He found the strip a bit difficult to locate amidst the hills, and was unhappy with his first landing at what was to be called Paddington Strip. These temporary strips were given the names of English railway stations, and the one next door would be called Waterloo.

It was on this day that unlike Ray, leaning outside, Smithy was sitting inside his tent doodling, awaiting the arrival of tea time, when several Focke-Wulfe 190s appeared. 'Quite a scene,' he wrote, as they dive-bombed the aerodrome, whilst like others around him, hell-bent on cover, he made for the nearest hill.

A flooded tent, with soaked kit bag and oozing mud surrounding their bunks, awaited everyone when returning from the field on the 17th. Arising the day after brought little improvement, with still no water, just slippery mud. News permeated down from the Flight Office that the C/O Jackie Sing had been hit by flak, and that after being damaged by enemy fighters Sgt Drinkwater had crash landed inside our lines. The good news in the afternoon was the sight of Drinkwater returning with his aircraft radio, plus a bit of debris from his Spit.

Len was airborne at the time flying number two to F/O Drummond, with everything going well, until the landing where Drummond upended his Spit onto its nose after finding a soft spot. Squadron rumours were now rife: they were to be made the first Spitfire bombing squadron. Groans echoed across the field.

The occupants of Len's tent decided a move would be appropriate, and this was accomplished on the 19th with excavations into the hillside, and better walling tackled by the adroit use of dirt-filled petrol cans. Typhus injections and the consumption of much fruit brought by an inmate from Setif ended the day, and Smithy had the temerity to complain once again of stomach pains.

The 20th dawned bright, and to cap it nicely, hot water was carried to their tent like manna from heaven. Another reconnaissance trip was all Smithy was allowed, but some of the squadron were out on Rhubarbs, leaving in pairs at two-minute intervals. The target was transport, a machine-gun nest, and any troops caught in the open. It was on this trip that Flight Sergeant

Birth of the Black Panthers

Roberts was brought down in flames, and there was no hope. Another of the lads, collecting several hits, did limp home.

Len sent mail to Blighty but was unhappy at not receiving any from our three sisters or myself.

This was the day, the 21st, that pilots were seconded to Setif to collect the new Spit bombers, leaving Smithy the dubious task of removing the current aircraft from dispersal to the far side of the field. Having first enjoyed an unusual lie-in, and fêted with double eggs at breakfast, Len found himself merrily humming a tune, nicely ensconced in one of the Spits, and about midway across the field.

It was at this precise moment that the air raid gun sounded off.

Others were already scampering for cover, but luckily, being only five feet nine and a half inches tall, and extremely muscular and athletic, Len managed to beat them by a head. Lying there half-buried he couldn't help reminiscing how the contrails high overhead reminded him of the Battle of Britain. As mud dried to the consistency of concrete, the heat became unbearable, vaguely he remembered some type commenting that this valley was called the Death Valley for white men – he could well believe the sentiments and prayed we would win before the dread midsummer heat drove everyone mad.

As he mulled the concept over in his mind for the first time he encountered Ray's bombs. Like the rest of the squadron he felt somewhat apprehensive when visualising the thought of lifting off with those extra 500 pounds of high explosive dangling beneath the wings. Quickly coming to terms, however, he committed to his diary in boyish fashion that the first time he embarked on a mission he was going to write on the deadly casing, 'An Eye for an Eye, and Tooth for a Tooth'. It was his humble opinion that Jerry would get a big shock when Spits actually dropped them.

These developments were not going to be all that pleasant for our Johnny either. Ray takes up the story in his very informative and detailed audio tapes.

The configuration for attachment of the bombs comprised an electromagnetic release beneath each wing, with four pre-drilled fibre pads two aft and two forward of this release mechanism. Into these went four metal stays, or rods, two of which being adjustable. The opposite ends of these rods slotted into four holes previously drilled in the actual bomb.

This in itself was fine, but the holes in each bomb had to be drilled by the armourers in the dead of night.

Enough bombs for the following day's missions had to be got ready. Maximum missions per day could be six, with the whole squadron taking part. In other words 144 bombs with each one set on a jig to allow for correct alignment and drilled four times.

On one particular night as he sweated over this task, his drill accidentally went too deep, causing high explosive material to spiral up the drill, akin to wood shavings. One of the armourer's mates, busily rolling up the beasts for Ray's attention before removing the completed ones, stopped to enquire of this substance now escaping from the bomb. Quite naturally Johnnie obliged his inquisitor with the truth, which sent the poor erk scurrying for his life. Ray swears he never paused for breath for at least two miles.

By the 24th March Len had still not seen action, but, consistently anxious to keep his hand in, he did manage an evening flight, which failed to help his ego when B Flight's commander bawled him out for a b-awful split-arsed landing, threatening to drum him out of the service should he ever see the like again. Inwardly Smithy was seething, for his accuser, he reckons, has performed worse.

Little action materialised over the next few days, except on the 30th some of the boys were lucky enough to use their bombs, sending some enemy transport skywards. A pilot called Leque was shot down behind enemy lines but they reckoned he was okay. To cheer everyone up somebody spread the rumour that Turkish brass hats were inspecting tomorrow. 'Bags of Bull' was to be the order of the day.

It had reached the 2nd April and Len wrote:

Today Stan Glover and myself had the day off, so having nothing to do decided we'd see the front line. We got to Sedjenine, by hitch hiking taking about four hours. This place had only been taken by the army two days previous so we were on the right road to souvenirs, getting near the front line we found Flt Sgt Roberts machine up on the hill where it crashed sometime ago, the machine was in bits Robbie being buried by the side of his machine, buried by the Germans it looked like, on the grave was some photo's of his sisters which I think was good of the Jerries to leave there. We went on further passing dead mules that had been blown up by shell fire and just left at the side of the road, the road was one mass of shell holes and the trees on either side were just lumps of broken wood stuck in the ground. Moving further on we got to find out that way up on one of the hills was a German camp that the army had wiped out half an hour previous so after much climbing arrived at this place seeing four German soldiers sneaking in the bush. We didn't open fire seeing that we only had .38s against which might have been machine guns now that the jerries were trying to make their way back to their lines. We entered one of the huts to find much booty. I collected all told one luger automatic, underpants, four shirts, one pair of pants short, and bags of 9mm ammunition. Stan collecting about the same plus one potato masher which I think was worth risking.

Coming back riding on top of the lorry in case of enemy fighters I was nearly knocked down by a wire stretching across the road. This wasn't the end of the journey, on getting near Bega a 109 machine gunned the road killing two drivers behind us, myself being by this time in a hole twenty yards from the road which I made in two seconds beating all records, Stan making it in one ended up the day telling the boys some line shoots.

There was definitely a feeling of the quiet before the storm during this first week of April, and by the 7th Len found himself sitting alone in the middle of the field with the sun beating on his forehead, his mind full of sentiment and nostalgia. He commits to his diary:

Each day has been the same hot by day, damn cold at night. I think its time I described this valley to you.

Looking towards the south there's a stretch of mountains that go east as far as the eye can see, hills opposite are green with black patches, then going more east they get higher and become rockier

The sky above is blue, a pure Mediterranean blue, and everything is so quiet a quietness that makes one think of what's around you, and brings thoughts of loved ones at home, which is miles away, and then back to the war. It seemed funny with such quiet and peacefulness, with the mountains showing white against the blue sky. Nobody would ever think of war, until the silence of a Spitty starting up, followed by others, then with clouds of dust rising from the take off brings the mind back again. Finally everything settles once more to normal with the Spitty's now black specs in the distance, just above those white rocky-mountains. Twelve in all, twelve, I wonder how many I shall count when they return.

This goes on nearly every day, coming away from the drome about seven o'clock with only one thing in mind. To eat and then try to think of something different to do afterwards.

Len was unable to make a diary entry again until the 14th, as it happened, his birthday. On the 10th they were scrambled, this time under the command of F W 'Freddie' Lister DFC. The target forty-plus Junkers Ju 87s and Bf 109s above Medjez and Beja, but unfortunately the Jerries high-tailed it for their base before an attack could be pressed home.

By the 12th 152 was out in force bombing the village of Chouigui, just a cluster of some ten houses that the Germans had commandeered. Len's bombs landed twenty yards short of the mark, but he did score with machine-gun and cannon, before sweeping home right on the deck.

Scrambled again over Beja on the 13th, which proved unlucky, with so much dust and dirt thrown up by the propellers, visibility on take off could be next to nil, on this occasion causing two planes to collide. Sgt Drinkwater managed to escape with minor injuries. Unfortunately P/O Wallace, who Len describes as a very nice fellow, was killed.

This day they also lost Puzze, one of Len's tent companions. They had been escorting Yankee bombers when they were jumped by 109s. Puzze's machine received several hits, yet somehow he managed to get back over our lines and called up to say he was going to bail out, but he never made it, and his Spit was seen to go in vertically.

Len's flight had been given the task of escorting Hurricane bombers trying to dislodge some enemy infantry holding a strategic hill, which Len reckoned they succeeded in doing.

Four days later there was another collision, but no record of the outcome, and one likes to think that in this instance all was well.

Scrambled to 21,000 feet after enemy aircraft were sighted over Paddington Strip on the 18th April, they were once again too late to intercept, leaving everyone cursing their luck.

By late afternoon Len sat strapped into his cockpit following instructions to remain at readiness. His watch showed nearly four pm, a time reckoned by Ray to be favoured by the German Luftwaffe for attack. Sure enough they came streaking in dead on cue, Focke-Wulf 190s carrying bombs.

Len had already vacated his machine, legging it for cover, only to be scolded by his Flight Commander to 'get back in your perishing plane and stay there'! Dutifully Smithy obeyed, sitting there watching his irate commander bury himself in the ground for safety.

Fifteen minutes later they were given the all clear for take off, ordered to sweep near Tunis itself. The worst forty-five minutes Len said he'd experienced. Fired at by flak no matter which way they turned. His number one was unable to climb due to lack of power, so the only direction was down. Spotting a gun emplacement firing at his number one, immediately he tripped his own button, sending a four-second burst towards the defenders, silencing them and saving his friend.

Both planes then streaked for home at ground level, watching enemy troops run for their lives.

It was about this time that Ray says they were suddenly ordered in the middle of the night to start loading transport with ammo belts, starter batteries etc. for the express purpose of vacating camp. Where to and for what reason nobody knew. Suddenly, as swiftly as the orders had been issued they were withdrawn, leaving types cursing and cussing and wondering what the hell was happening.

By morning all could be revealed, apparently seizing an opportunity where our line was weakest, and held only by inexperienced American army units. General von Arnim, the German commander, had decided to break through at the Kasserine Pass area. A ploy if it could be completed successfully that would leave all the forward based squadrons wide open to encirclement. Without doubt a last ditch attempt to stem the inevitable, ever since Montgomery had broken through the Mareth line. This time the First Army were rushed in to stem the gap, and everyone could breathe a little easier, but it had been a close run thing.

Hitler's main concern was a holding action to enable as many personnel and their equipment to escape to Sicily, where he would make a bigger and better stand.

Involved in two trips on the 21st April looking for Stuka dive-bombers on the first and escorting 'Hurribombers' on the second, Len said they had a rookie pilot with them experiencing flak for the first time which unnerved him somewhat.

By the 30th they'd had a busy week, with Len too tired even to make diary entries, later he wrote:

The big push has started pushing Jerry back mile by mile this being well supported by the RAF of course we doing our share or I should say more than our share, being as we are the only spit bomber squadron, on some of the trips we went as fighters on one of these on the 29th the squadron was called to do Rhubarbs on German trucks two a/c going out at two minute intervals, it was on this day through Rhubarbs we lost four aircraft two pilots I believe being killed Sgt Utterson and F/O Drummond two of the best fellows in the squadron the other two returning two days later from the hospital. This same day F/Sgt Spire and myself were pranging two Jerry trucks when we were jumped by two ME109s one trying to get on my tail F/Sgt Spire seeing this turned on him while I manoeuvred out of the way also keeping an eye on the other ME109 above which came down getting behind Spire who was by now pooping at his Jerry. I couldn't say anything to Spire in case he turned into his sights so I in turn turned onto this Jerry giving a five second burst of machine gun and cannon fire until I saw him go down in flames through a cloud. By this time Spire had seen the red hot tracers coming at him had done a half roll and when on the bottom saw my ME hit the ground and blow up. We came home right on the deck I doing a victory roll and when on landing was so excited I fell out of the machine.

The next day was the best day I think I shall remember, escorting Bostons we again got jumped by 109Gs from above. This turned into a dogfight which I think my spitty done things which I hope it will never do again. In this fight I damaged an ME which dived vertically after trying to get on my tail, in the dive I got a three second burst seeing hits on his wings.

As they entered the first week of May, so each day became similar to the last, with the squadron seeing much action.

Ray expressed similar sentiments, working round the clock as sortie followed sortie. 'Why!' he said, 'with the Eighth Army advancing steadily westwards, preceded by the Afrika Korps and the First Army creeping ever nearer Tunis, the Bizerta and Cape Bon areas were beginning to look like Anfield on an important match day.'

Certainly the Germans were becoming bottled up, fighting a fierce rearguard action, with upwards of 150,000 troops battling it out for as much time as possible. By the 7th May our armies were marching into Tunis, where just prior to this 152 had hammered Tunis Aerodrome. Things had been a bit shaky but Len did manage to drop both bombs on a Me 323, a big six-engine transport.

Days before had been quite exciting too. On one trip the squadron was ordered to dive-bomb a German destroyer in the Gulf of Tunis, where three of the squadron's planes received hits from the destroyer's accurate flak. This left Sgt Spire, Len's number one, having to bail out. On this occasion Len had been next to last to go in, the ship's crew having got their range by now. He was lucky, although almost able to smell the cordite, his plane escaped damage as he pulled from the dive.

On 7th May 1943 Len's diary continues:

On another trip we went out to bomb some 52's near Tunis. On coming back we bumped into some 109's and 190's dive bombing our boys I was then at a height of 8000 feet seeing one of the 109's on the deck to starboard of me, I went down getting on his tail, he started to skid climb and turn trying to get me off his tail but my good old spitty held him while I pumped all my ammunition into him seeing hits over his a/c until getting near his base he burst into flames going over very slowly on his back to right himself and then went down very slowly towards some hills. By then we were at a height of 2000 feet, I was waiting to see him crash when I spotted six 109's diving on my starboard side having no ammunition I quickly turned for home not seeing my 109 crash so I only could claim a probable.

Quite a few of the boys were hit by flak and also bullets and cannon shells from 190's.

The Flight commander was hit also by a 190 who jumped him from behind.

The last trip today was very shaky, we went out to bomb the evacuation barges but the weather was against us having to fly nearly on the deck until a shower of tracer cannon shells came whistling up making the squadron turn about, for the first time I brought my bombs back being fired at on the way back by our on guns, got hit on the prop.

On the 8th May another ship was dive-bombed and Len reports a direct hit into its side, which he was convinced didn't do it any good, then back home strafing evacuation barges on the way.

Next day it was the Jerry airfields copping it again, with a direct hit by Smithy sending a Focke-Wulf 190 skywards, rounded off by raking the field with cannon and machine-gun fire.

Road transport was next, but this day, the 10th, saw Smithy pushing his piles somewhat. Bang over the target and the Spit developed a glycol leak, forcing him to watch his temperature rise as he nursed the plane down from 8000 feet. She gave up the ghost over Medjez, where a tug on the safety harness allowed him to do a wheels-up belly landing in a field alongside the highway. The most nerve-wracking part of this experience, he reported, was having to hitch a ride past lines of German prisoners of war. They hated airmen, he wrote, and he didn't blame 'em!

To keep everybody on the squadron posted of daily happenings each one would have a bulletin sheet, which surprisingly enough is not referred to by Ray, but fortunately Len happened to retain a couple throughout his service life, which I am able to quote from.

Called *The Paddington Post*, Volume 1, dated Tuesday May 4th, reads:

There was a shock awaiting Corporal Giles, our worthy Mess cook, when he awoke this morning, so much so indeed that he leapt from his pit with greater celerity than at one time thought possible. For lying next to him among the blankets was a snake of considerable size, in the process of attempting to swallow a frog!

This adventure of the cook was not unnaturally the chief subject of conversation at breakfast when despite the early hour F/Sgt Hubble summed up the situation with remarkable wit! "It was a bloody good thing" said Hubble "that the snake had a frog in its mouth"

Ps Corporal Giles agrees with him!

A Destroyer was reported by our aircraft on four separate occasions the other day as being just off the beach in Tunis Bay. The Navy was at once informed. "That's alright" came the reply "We already have that Rock charted!"

Wednesday 5th

Today was as exciting as any 152 has experienced recently. After dropping their bombs well and truly among Ju52's on Protville Airfield, they ran into some eight F.W.190s and their escort of 109's which had been bombing Tanks at Mateur.

In the ensuing dog fight Sgt Smith got a probable and Sgt Ash a damaged.

It was F/Lt Baynham's 13th bombing trip and it brought him mixed luck. Just when he was well on the tail of a 190 his cannons jammed, seconds later he heard sounds of bullets striking his aircraft, it was another 190, 50yds behind. He turned but the Hun turned with him getting in more shots which got his Glycol, and it was not until completing two more turns that he was able to shake the 190 off. His luck held, despite his damaged engine and rudder, making it safely back to base.

Americans today continued advancing and are now only ten miles from Bizerta. Enemy counter attacks with seventeen tanks in the Medjez area were repulsed with the loss of twelve including several Mark VI's.

Our Navy blew up a 6000ton-supply ship carrying munitions from Naples to Tunis, also sinking an escorting E Boat.

Thursday May 6th.

Ghurka Rifles brought over from the Eighth Army drive Huns from last strongholds in the hills around Medjez.

Thirty six sorties were carried out by 152 alone. Once the squadron was dived upon by unidentified aircraft, forcing B Flight to jettison their bombs before discovering the intruders were friendly.

One jettisoned bomb scored a direct hit on a farmhouse occupied by Jerry!

Caption Corner- Know your Hun!

Don't pull the chain or lift the seat until you are sure no unpleasant traps attached. It is surely better to miss the luxury and dig your own hole, than to end up in one!

Friday 7th
Great day for 152, after knocking hell out of aircraft on the ground at dreaded Aquina Airfield,

They followed up by visit to Protville, leaving three Ju 52s in flames.

In addition there were a number of Me323s, one bomb scoring a direct hit, which must have pushed Goerings piles somewhat!

Pilots pranging Ju52s were, The C/O, F/Lt Pocock, Sgts MacDonald, Glover and Dear. Glover also took a poop at a Siebel Ferry near the beach, but as he himself said he only had machine gun bullets left by that time.

Note! An Echelon tool-box, when opened this afternoon was found to contain a Bees nest among the tools! Further comment is superfluous.

Saturday 8th
152 carried bombs to the most easterly aerodromes of Tunisia, not only dropping them among the dispersed aircraft, but chasing and shooting down two Me109s, which had just taken off. One of these was shared by F/Lt Baynham and F/O Tooth. Chasing him across country firing in turn until seeing him crash land at high speed in the foot hills west of Keliba.

Sgt Glover chased the other scoring hits around the cockpit hood, probably wounding the pilot. The last Glover saw was as it rolled slowly onto its back only ten feet above the waves, unable to watch any longer for at that moment he was attacked by the Huns number two.

More fun was in store for 152 when making their third visit over the Hun lines this evening. On Menzel Temine Airfield they found at least a dozen Ju52's, as well as several single engined aircraft. Of these they left at least four in flames. The C/O got two of the flamers, and Sgt Smith got a direct hit with a bomb on a Focke Wolf 190, altogether it was a first class show.

Our troops have received a tremendous welcome from the people of Tunis, streets were strewn with flowers as they marched in.

Birth of the Black Panthers

Sunday 9th

When 152 went out early this morning they could find nothing worth bombing, and so perforce brought their bombs back, all that is except Killer Kingsford, who pissed off on his own out to sea, and finding a 40ft Schooner with 70 to 100 men aboard, proceeded to drop both bombs in the middle of it. After having first shot off the mast with his cannon, there seems little doubt that every Hun aboard can be counted as confirmed.

Later the squadron was out again, shooting up transport, each aircraft making two runs along the length of the convoy. On this trip F/Lt Baynham had trouble with his oil pressure, and Sgt Smith had to land at Medjez with an internal Glycol leak.

Advertisement section!
Piles !!!!!!!!!- Consult Messrs Baynham and Smith—Medjez Telegrams; Glycol

Monday May 10th

Hit by flak in the engine, the C/O of 152 made a good crash landing not far east of Tunis. The rest of the squadron seeing him climb out of his aircraft sent messages of encouragement over the R/T- not without some jealousy at the thought of the party in Tunis that evening.

There is now apart from flak, no opposition to our air offensive.

At the conclusion of the fighting in the battle areas to the north of Tunis, it is reported that 50,000 prisoners have been taken and that numbers will increase considerably. It is interesting to note that among those captured were three Divisional Generals and Staff, also the entire 15th Panzer Division which surrendered en-bloc!

Meanwhile the Navy now operate freely along the whole Tunisian coastline, ready to deal with any Hun attempting to get away.

And within the last throes of this campaign, the final paragraph upon preciously preserved *Paddington Post* paper is this:

A pilot crash landing on the recently captured airfield at Ferryville, when asked by an admiring French helper if scratches on his nose were caused by the prang, replied!

"No" They were caused by thorns from all the Roses everyone threw at me!

Two days later it was all over, General von Arnhim and over 200,000 other prisoners were in the Allies' hands – the rest had either fled or were dead. To the victor go the spoils, this truism certainly held sway after the Tunisian campaign, not for gold or riches, nor a harem full of beautiful girls. No! what everybody now had after fighting through sinking mud, then choking dust, was running hot and cold water and concrete runways, not to mention the delightful, the luxurious, the sensuous all embracing Mediterranean Sea.

Thousands of naked bodies now plunged into her inviting waters.

The squadron's new base was Protville, that old enemy stronghold from which all the Focke-Wulf 190 fighter bombers had set out to destroy the Allies' temporary strips.

Len was excited to find one or two 190s still intact, left behind in the hurried German withdrawal. I have been unable to find a record appertaining to it, but at the time he was expressing hopes of being able to fly one just as soon as they were made serviceable.

Ray tells of visiting the wondrous ruins of Carthage, that venue of conflict from another time, where alongside a couple of thousand other service personnel 152 frolic'd in the altogether, swimming, and basking on the sand. 'It's during this time,' he chuckled, 'a Jeep cruised straight along the crowded beach, carrying Yank officers escorting two very attractive females. Neither them nor us turned a hair,' said Ray.

Ray's narrative continued:

Soon the Spits took off for Malta with me and the rest of the ground crew, including all our ordnance, transport, cookhouse, admin etc., embarking on landing craft. It was like moving house except you took the house as well.

All transport had now been modified to cope with the surf,' he said, 'allowing them to drive straight up the lowered ramps of the flat bottomed boats.

Birth of the Black Panthers

After arriving at Valletta Harbour, everyone was quickly moved up to an airfield at Ta-Kali, where the squadron again continued to operate as Spit bombers until such time as the Allies invaded Sicily. Only then would they quickly revert to fighters, enabling them to give better cover to the Allied invasion forces.

Being the month of June the first impression fixed in Ray's mind as each set foot on new home ground, was how magnified the heat and light from the sun seemed to be, bouncing as it did off all the numerous white stone buildings.

Their billet was to be empty houses positioned along the sea front at Selima, looking for all the world like an English seaside resort. Unfortunately that's where the resemblance ended, for with Malta fast becoming one huge jumping off post, the water supply couldn't cope. Consequently it had become very brackish, not only awful to drink, but decidedly unpleasant to cook with, making their food taste foul. Still compared to Smithy's, Ray's arrival on Malta had been pretty uneventful.

Like everyone else stationed at Protville, Len had headed for the beach, joining in with several other pilots from 152. They even decided to stop there after so many journeys back and forth to their new base.

Receiving word that the squadron was on the move again, they knew not where, it was agreed that if they nipped back quick and packed their kites first with all their usual bits and pieces, they might just make it in time to catch an ENSA show being given for our victorious lads.

Len takes up the story.

It was while we were piling on the miles per hour coming back, that a twerp of a driver driving in the opposite direction decides to pull out in front of us making us swerve catching him with our wing to send us skidding head on into another truck. I being in the front saw what was going to happen so getting up in the seat having in mind to jump over the top of the lorry when we hit. I'm afraid this didn't work it happened to soon, I did go out but the windscreen was in my way which didn't stop there very long, I then found myself sailing through the air with a few other bods, then a nasty thud making me pass into the valley of birds. Nick died when I came too, he looked just the same as when he was asleep with a smile on his face, Ash died on the way to hospital I felt his pulse which was very slow then his eyes rolled back I think he broke his neck, Jack the last person died in hospital, the rest of us were put in there for bruises and cuts. Ace was very funny to look at one half of his pants being torn off showing his bot. Coming out of hospital we found the Sqd had gone so we just hung around our old spot by the sea wondering what we should do next, it was then we found out where our Sqd had gone which was Malta a few more inquiries put us hitchhiking on the road to Matour there to catch a D.C.3. We arrived to see the D.C. take off, I could have cried the heat was terrific and the flies and nothing to eat we found out again there was another D.C.3. going the next day so we stopped the night having to sleep under the stars, then the rain in the night getting soaked that was the end so this was life. The next day saw us 3000feet above and heading away from the god forsaken place, a couple of hours went by and then Malta was sighted, then the landing then to our Sqd which was at another drome on the island. We hitchhiked there giving a girl a lift on the way and she spoke English. What a different man I am now, happy as a skylark.

They guessed why the squadron had been sent to Malta, but for a short while at least it was going to be flicks, dancing and swimming, plus of course larking about with one or two girls.

Ray would start to live it up too, describing the red light district of Valletta. 'The infamous street,' he said, 'was called the Gut.' But they did find a decent bar there, which enjoyed their patronage, called The Greyhound.

Close to Ta Kali airstrip ('well nothing was ever that far away on the Island') stood the town of Mosta, whose cathedral supported one of the largest domes in the world. It was a place Ray visited, to see for himself where during the siege of Malta a German unexploded bomb had penetrated the dome, crashing into the pews below.

On the 15th June Len took off again for a recce over their sector, he hadn't flown since his last patrol above destroyers at Cape Bon on the 19th May. By the 18th June he was with the squadron sweeping over Sicily, spying five Focke-Wulfe 190s, but the enemy kept well clear. On the 19th he was helping in the search for aircrew downed in the Med, but no luck. After a couple more uneventful sweeps, by the 28th he was again back on bombing missions, this time a salt factory at Licata and another near Comiso. He describes it as follows:

There were a few habitable buildings close by, this is the first time we have been called upon for a target like this, I had a few hours to think it over, women and children coming to mind! There hadn't been any in Africa. The only thing to do was to go in at roof top to be sure of hitting it. This we did, diving nearly into the factory, pulling up to see my bombs go square in the middle.

I came out of the town, right over the riverbed, just missing the bridges, quite good fun.

The Comiso effort was good too when 109's came down after us, as we half rolled out.

Normally 109's can easily catch a Spit in a dive, but not with our bombs on.

Mac! was the only one to get shot up, having eight on his tail. I looked around after bombing but saw nothing but Spits, so coming back I rolled over the town just to show there were no hard feelings.

Top cover to Mitchell bombers attacking Catania on 7th July, meant that once more 152 were a fighter squadron. They did see a Macchi 202, who half rolled away, leaving no hope of catching him, also on this trip Sgt Armstrong had to bail out, but he was rescued okay.

The night before the Sicilian invasion on July 10th the squadron were out covering the barges.

'What a sight,' said Len; 'there seemed to be millions of boats going very slowly. It was giving him a feeling he couldn't quite explain, but he wondered how many of those chaps down there were going to come through.'

The next day everyone was cutting each other's throats to get airborne, Len getting his chance first thing in the morning, having to patrol the shoreline. He found it almost overwhelming, boats stretching as far as the eye could see, some burning, some already sunk, and others in the throes of sinking. Try as he might he could not spy any enemy aircraft which he found most strange, and difficult to fathom. Unfortunately some of the invasion fleet thought his flight were the enemy, often opening up thereby setting off other boats in the area. Len wrote:

What a barrage they put up. But was I mad, the silly tits! can't they see we're Spits.

We did this patrol at night as well, which I thought was going a bit far, having to cross the sea, and running into red hot bursts from our own ships, all very pretty, but!

It was an amazing sight to see the Warships firing at the island, to follow a white hot shell screaming over the coastline and watch it burst some distance inland

It was while observing one of these that a 109 came up behind me, catching sight of his white spinner in the moonlight I turned to attack, forcing him to dive, until I lost him in the darkness, having to go back home all by myself, just guessing the direction with an anxious eye on my fuel gauge, which was getting damn low, too low to miss Malta. But lady luck was with me and I had steered the right course.

By mid July three-quarters of 152's ground crew received one hour's notice to pack and be ready to move. They were to embark on landing craft that would take them to the port of Syracuse. The remainder including Ray would stay for the time being to service the Spits, before they too flew to Sicily.

It was during this period that things began hotting up. Firstly, although I do not have their names or any idea of their fate, Len writes that three of the boys were shot down, having been jumped by 109s.

Secondly, Len did get a chance when a stooge of a convoy patrol came up, and A and B Flights tossed for it with B Flight winning, thereby leaving Len's A flight with the thankless task. Ray tells of the account by remembering six Italian aircraft being shot down, but we will follow Smithy's description as an eyewitness.

The patrol was just off Augusta, two rather big ships, and a few smaller ones. After being out there ten minutes turning round to give another run across the convoy I spotted a bomb go off in the water looking up to see aircraft diving I then turned diving down to catch one of them going right down on the deck flat out and catching up on what turned out to be a Reggio 2000, I closed right in on him giving a five second burst, he then tried to turn but I'm afraid I hit him again seeing my cannon knock his aircraft to pieces, his wing went down catching the sea making him go straight in. I then turned around to see Roy firing at another but missing. I covered him until he ran out of ammunition then I told him I'd take over, closing in on this a/c I opened fire seeing hits on his wing and then his hood blow up with a cannon shell right inside. The aircraft just seemed to fall to pieces I running right into some of these causing damage to my aircraft, he then turned and went straight in his tail came up then went slowly under, coming back we had found out the four of us had knocked down six out of eight aircraft which pushed B flights piles seeing us do the victory rolls.

The actual victors were Smithy one and half, F/O Roy Kingsford one and half, and F/O Jones three.

No. 152's Spitfires flew to Sicily on the 21st July, leaving Ray and the remaining ground crew after seeing their charges safely off, to follow as quickly as possible by sea to the port of Augusta, with everyone finally being re-united at an airstrip called Lentini East on the 24th. This airstrip was near the coast inside the Bay of Catania, and to the south of the city bearing the same name. Mount Etna reared up to the north and General Montgomery's caravan was sited just outside their domestic quarters.

According to Len the front line was only three miles away, so regularly at 10:00 pm you couldn't sleep for the Allied gunners pounding away at Catania, with explosions lighting up the night sky. Now and again, so Ray tells us, Monty would bump into the lads, stopping to offer them cigarettes and ask after their welfare, which helped to bolster their morale.

There was a small river close by, which each time it curved into a bend, increased in depth to at least four feet, making it ideal for the lads to enjoy a swim in fresh water. They would cavort in this each evening, until one time as darkness approached somebody spied a snake whipping across the surface, types couldn't scramble up the bank fast enough. After that it was back to the sea again, only this time they had to run the gauntlet of Jerry minefields, gingerly treading past tempting grapevines and deep sand dunes to stay inside the sappers tape. There was however a watermelon field nearby which appeared habitable, probably because the enemy had needed the sustenance themselves; now it was 152's turn.

With 152 no longer operating as a bombing squadron, the powers that be whisked Freddie Lister back to Blighty. Preparations were afoot for the invasion of France and Freddie was obviously going to be the man to forge further bombing operations with Spitfires. How I came to discover the next episode of Freddie's life was truly remarkable, when a friend loaned me his library book called *Spitfire Diary*. The author was our namesake, a certain Ted Smith, now a resident of Austin in Texas, a British Spitfire pilot who flew with Freddie from D-Day onwards. After reading his book in 1994, I managed to contact Ted who, first giving me Freddie's address and phone number, then informed me that Freddie's parents had owned the Southampton ice rink before the war, and that Freddie had been a champion barrel jumper on ice skates, and at one time even been in line for possible gold in the Olympics.

His new squadron was to be No. 127, which distinguished itself throughout the second front and beyond. All its pilots loved Freddie, who after the war held regular binges at his home in Lincolnshire for ex-127 pilots until his unfortunate demise a short time after I'd managed to speak with him over the telephone. Although that opportunity was very special to me, dear Freddie was unable to recall Smithy.

Ray remembers that the day after everyone had joined up at Lentini, Wing Commander C F Gray paid them a visit. He was the Winco in charge of the three squadrons at Lentini, and indicated that this day he would lead the wing from 152. It was to be a momentous day and one which Len initially cursed because, not scheduled for Ops, he missed it.

News had come through the Y service that a whole gaggle of Ju 52 transports were heading across the Messina Straits, covered by supporting 109s. Len said, 'The Winco flew everyone right on the deck in the Straits to avoid the German Y service getting the DF[4] on them.'

The heading given turned out to be spot on with the Junkers sighted at sea level to port. Before the guarding Bf 109s could get at them the squadrons sailed in, sending Ju 52s exploding and crashing into the sea all over the place. Ray's reports indicated that at least twenty-nine Ju 52s were destroyed, ten of which were claimed by 152 plus two 109s which were accounted for by F/O Jones. 152 Squadron pilots credited were the Winco two, F/L Baynham one and a half, F/O Roy Kingsford two plus a probable, F/O Jones two and a half, F/O Borrows and P/O Macdonald one shared, Sgt Bradbury two, Flt Sgt Patterson one.

One pilot would be lost, F/O Reg Marshall was believed to have scored a

4 detailed fix

victory before having to bail out. His parachute was last seen heading towards a burning patch of sea where one of the Junkers had gone in. F/O Marshall hailed from Auckland, New Zealand, and was initially reported missing, but later presumed dead.

From the outcome both Len and Ray were of the opinion that quite a few if not all of these Ju 52s must have been carrying petrol, as when hit they quickly caught fire. It must have been a desperate situation for the German crews.

But hearing of another sortie in the afternoon similar to the last, Len couldn't get airborne quickly enough. He takes up the story.

Again the Sqd flew right on the deck I being this time Red four the second run down the straits 109's came down on us Jerry being wise my own section was turning to starboard when one 109 came in behind me, our section broke down while I broke into him which he half rolled and went straight down I turned then to find my No 1 seeing these two Spits chasing one 109 below to Port & another Spit which I thought was my No 1 chasing another 109 then from nowhere another 109 jumped this spit on my starboard I calling him up to break from which he did also the other spits on my Port. This action left me with 4 109's I picked the last one diving down on top of him, by this time we were just crossing Messina, Jerry being right on the deck by the time I was right on the top of him we were crossing the two mile stretch of sea between Sicily and Italy. Excitement did not make me think of my own skin and where I actually was I then gave him a 2 second burst seeing bursts over his cockpit and wing, overshooting him I pulled up and around to find that he had gone straight in the sea. Flak came up soon after this which made me think of POW after what seemed to me hours I got out of these straits and headed back home.

Two appendices to this day's activity were recorded by Ray. Firstly a diminutive unnamed Flying Officer pilot claimed that he never saw any enemy aircraft, which everybody put down to the fact that he probably couldn't see over the rim of the cockpit, and secondly that Flt Lt George Baynham returned with his parachute caught in his radiator gear.

A few nights after this momentous day Lentini airstrip became the centre of attention from Luftwaffe bombers. The raid signalled Ray's Ground Staff Commander, a certain Flt Sgt Flash Fenton, to speed by Jeep to the field, and with disregard to his own safety proceed to disperse as many of 152's Spits to the far corners as fast as humanly possible. The brave effort later earned Flt Sgt Fenton a mention in dispatches.

Tomatoes were extremely plentiful at this time of year, a delight that found its way into every menu. The method described by Ray was to boil them in a large zinc bath which the cook assured them was definitely not used for any other purpose.

On August 4th Len kept cover for a Walrus flying boat which successfully rescued a downed pilot in Catania Bay. A Mustang pilot had a lucky escape on the 5th when Len recognised the Bf 109 look-a-like just in time.

Things began to quieten down a little after this, and Sicily fell to the Allies on the 17th August. It was time for Ray and the boys to do a bit of sightseeing, visiting the airfield at Catania, and nosing around for souvenirs. The 'drome was a large permanent affair, and among other things Ray managed to lay his hand on some interesting photographs. Each one had a large official mark, bearing the stamp of the Regia Aeronautica, looking for the entire world like medal presentations. Others were definitely funeral processions of German airmen. To this day these are part of Ray's memorabilia.

Describing a gully running under the main east coast road south of Catania, which in winter would in all probability be a fast torrent of water, Ray paints the picture of past battles. The area is quite close to Lentini and the bridge at this point was a scene of heavy fighting. Many graves littered the land, and a German 88 mm gun was still in evidence. Rumour had it that the Yorkshire and England cricketer Hedley Verity was mortally wounded here and later succumbed to these wounds whilst being held in an Italian prisoner of war camp.

Towards the end of August Len did get another poop, as he described it,[5] at a couple of 109s, but no luck. His logbook does tell us however that 'Sparky went straight in'. I am afraid that I have been unable to establish further the identity of this gallant gentleman.

There appears to be a slight variation on the actual date of our invasion of the Italian mainland, with Ray plumping for the 2nd and Smithy for the 3rd September 1943. It was probably during the late night and early morning of both. Whichever was the case Montgomery's Eighth Army swept across

---

5 *Poop* was a well used word of the 1940s, meaning to shoot.

the Straits of Messina to land on Italy's toe at Reggio Calabria.

On the 9th the Fifth Army, comprising equal numbers of British and American troops, landed at Salerno, about thirty miles south of Naples, and to help cover this new foothold 152 moved nearer the action.

Once more the squadron had a new commanding officer, this time a New Zealander, Sqn Ldr Bruce Ingram DFC, whose father as a matter of interest was Dunedin's Fire Brigade Chief. Bruce and Smithy were destined to become great friends.

The new airfield was to be a dustbowl near the town of Milazzo, on Sicily's northern coast, just west of Messina. From here, armed with the latest Spitfire Mk IXs carrying ninety-gallon overload tanks, 152 would be performing long range sweeps in support of the Salerno beachhead.

The actual strip location happened to be very close to the spot where all those Ju 52s had been encountered, and Len said their flight times and distances to Salerno were pretty shaky dos. It is hard to imagine today with modern air travel, but to our pilots having to travel 170 miles before being able to carrying out your sweep, and then back again to base, meant having to sit and possibly fight cramped up in a tiny cockpit for three and a quarter hours. Shot at by who knows who from who knows where. Duration over the target area was down to a mere twenty to twenty-five minutes. To cap it all, complained Len, 'throughout this whole time the Squadron only bagged one 109 and damaged another'. But the sight had been amazing, not unlike the invasion of Sicily, accept these were much smaller boats darting to and fro.

The move to Milazzo for Ray and his friends had been quite impressive, travelling by road round the western slopes of Mount Etna, sometimes stopping to stretch their legs affording the opportunity to inspect the desolate spectacle of ancient lava flows. One pertinent point, as reported by Ray, brought gasps of incredulity, when local inhabitants informed them quite casually that their next port of call would be Salerno – and this was before the Allies had landed. It made everyone wonder, when the attack took place, if perhaps lack of secrecy were not the reason for the huge German build up. For one horrible moment, as Ray and the rest of the world knew, it was definitely touch and go.

Two pilots were to be lost at Milazzo, one being Flt Lt Dreski. It can be very difficult sometimes to obtain true facts: for fifty years I had always interpreted his name in Len's writings as 'Drake', and his version of events tells of this officer swerving on take-off, because of the terrible dusty conditions, and striking a PR (photo reconnaissance) Spitty. (Conditions, Len says, were so bad he once had to take off using instruments only.) In 1999, I had the good fortune to speak with a nephew of this Polish officer, a man by the name of Tom Dreski, when I was trying to assist this gentleman with the history of his uncle. Tom told me that in actual fact his uncle had experienced a tyre blow-out which had been the cause of the catastrophe. In either case, as Len said, poor Dreski didn't stand a chance with that ninety-gallon fuel tank slung under the belly of his Spit.

The other pilot who died at Milazzo was Flt Sgt Pettit, one of the best said Smithy. They lost him on one of the sweeps: he just disappeared into thin air apparently, nobody ever seeing him again

'It was the next day,' Smithy wrote; 'They landed in Italy, or rather, arrived, for the Runway was just off the sea running from east to west, and only 700yds long.' He continued:

Balloons were flying from the barges on the sea shore, leaving a clearance for us to land; further out at sea was the Rodney and Nelson firing a salvo every two minutes across the aerodrome to the hills beyond. The other end was the army doing likewise, to tell you the truth I thought this was the end making my approach just over the boundary these guns opened up giving a rather loud noise also a violent bump making my landing rather fast just missing a ditch at the other end, if I had of gone down there I would have kept three other guys company.

That evening I met Mac of 232 sitting down on a tree log eating our tea when three shells came whistling across injuring one fellow in the foot this wasn't the end the Luftwaffe had come over and give us a welcome mingled with some more shells. That night was the worst I'd spent ever.

The next morning we went down to the drome having to wait a quarter of an hour before take off. That quarter of an hour was spent in the ditch owing to FW190's dive bombing the place in between these raids we managed to get off the deck. F/O Jones and myself being in Spit 9s top cover to the fives. Coming along the beach for the fourth time FW190's again tried to bomb the shipping I'm afraid we couldn't stop them bombing but we breathed freely when they missed all this time of course Jones and myself were going down vertically after these buggers I saw one on the deck about a thousand yards in front covering 20 miles doing a speed of 460 mph before getting anywhere near him, at 600 yds we passed over our drome flak opening up on this Hun but missing and coming pretty close to me. In the end we were right on the deck coming to some hills the silly tit instead of going round the hill tried to get over the top allowing me to give everything I'd got instead he hit it and made a bloody mess of himself pieces going for miles.

Meanwhile their ground crews had once again travelled by sea, this time in tank landing craft. 'Thankfully the journey went without incident,' says Ray, although as they beached some shelling was taking place. One assumes this was the same Allied artillery and naval exchange experienced by Len, although Ray also jokingly ventures the theory that the enemy were using laser controlled bombs from high flying aircraft. On the way over he recalls seeing the Lipari Islands, and the volcanic mountain of Stromboli rearing, so it appeared, straight from the surface of the sea.

I met Flying Officer (later Flight Lieutenant) Jones at Ray's eightieth birthday party, a sprightly upright figure of a man with sparkling eyes. 'We were the original "Smith and Jones",' he said.

Len reckoned they were really in the war front here, at night, in between the shelling they could hear the rattle of machine-guns in the hills. He was quite convinced that the squadron landed too soon, as there was a big tank battle going on just to the south of them. The strip at Salerno, as you can imagine, was quite close to the beach, called Asa, taking its name from the nearby river. Squadron duties were to protect our lines of communication and keep enemy activity to a minimum.

There wasn't much time for Ray and the other three hundred-odd ground staff to enjoy themselves. He recalls being billeted in a tobacco factory, of all places, about a mile from the strip. This venue had recently been the scene of fierce fighting, but huge stacks of tobacco leaves still permeated the air, wafting their pungent aroma as they went through various stages of curing.

Not far from the strip Ray used to pass an orange and lemon grove, discreetly helping himself to a dozen of the latter to stuff at the base of his kit bag. 'Then I promptly forgot all about the damn things,' he laughs.

Meanwhile for Len flying and fighting were still the norm. 'We were bound to see something sooner or later,' he wrote:

We did, this time the whole of the squadron having a do, this time the buggers didn't drop their bombs, forcing them to jettison them in the hills.

We piled into them, I getting right on top of a couple of these, but only firing a few rounds both cannons being jammed up, but before they jammed one guy went back home with a couple holes in him.

Gee! was I mad, I had that guy sitting pretty, my machine guns worked, but they sound silly after the cannon, so I just gave up having a mind to tear a strip off those serving Commando's, but this wasn't necessary the C/O being in the same plight as myself.

I learned in later years that cannon could be prone to this phenomenon, so it would be churlish to cast a shadow on Ray or his colleagues.

One morning in late September 1943 everyone was on the move again, this time to an airfield still in the Salerno area called Serretella. They were destined not to remain long; in fact Ray never made it at all, being part of an advance party routed via Naples to where the squadron was supposedly going to end up. Len's log does tell of a flight from Serretella on 1st October taking place over northeast Salerno, with the cryptic message, 'One Bridge Busted', With a further entry on the 13th: 'Patrol Naples, Damn cold'.

In the meantime Ray struck out by road, leaving the plains of Salerno behind to trundle over the hills towards the Bay of Naples. The journey and weather were pleasant enough but the signs of war remained evident everywhere.

Soon after leaving Salerno they passed through the town of Batapaglia, hosting one of Italy's main railway junctions and marshalling yards. The place was an abysmal shambles, completely twisted and gutted, overwhelmed by aerial bombardment. Ray stared in awe at man's destructiveness, yet not far from this devastation, as tired dishevelled bodies peered from their trucks, what should they see but an elegantly dressed distinguished looking elderly gent, rolled up newspaper under one arm, with an equally elegantly dressed attractive young blonde on the other as though both were out for a Sunday afternoon stroll.

They couldn't believe it, says Ray; imagine such a scene as this in the middle of so much carnage.

Soon they left the plains behind them and could look down on Naples Bay, commanded by Mount Vesuvius on the one side, and azure sea edged by small fishing villages on the other. Strange little places, Ray recalls fondly, that now, he says, figure prominently in all the holiday travel brochures.

Stopping briefly at Pompeii to allow everyone to stretch their legs, they could easily have entered the ruins. All the turnstiles had been abandoned, which is not surprising considering the Germans had only just vacated the place. Retreating so fast there was still an anti-tank gun complete with ammunition stuck in the entrance.

They finally let everyone offload, dropping them next to a building looking very much like a school, which would serve as their billet, except hardly had they unpacked then it was as you were, and back on the road again.

The powers that be were surpassing themselves as far as Ray was concerned, but at least they did get a little time to look over Naples. The city looked awful; a sorry sight indeed, before they'd left the Germans had sabotaged the water supply, leaving the poor Italian civilians wandering aimlessly searching for help. One must remember that since the successful taking of Sicily, Mussolini had resigned and the Italian government and all its forces were now on the side of the Allies, so the Germans left no favours.

Wasting little time their wandering advance party (remember the bulk of the ground staff had gone to Serretella) discovered themselves a very nice Italian tuck shop. It was here that Ray and a couple of the lads enjoyed the friendliness of the owner and his wife, being plied not just with sweetmeats but good wine. It wasn't long before invitations stretched to dining in the back room, where for a couple of hours said Ray we were offered various bottles to sample. Neither the owner nor his wife would hear of any payment so all one could do to repay such hospitality was hand over all the cigarettes they could muster.

'Needless to say,' says Ray, 'the boys and I were floating on air!'

Surprisingly they did not strike out north next day, but turned away from the fighting, heading southeast to go over the Apennine Mountains. Temperatures at altitude in early October could be decidedly chilly especially when one considers just a short time earlier everyone had been sweltering in the eighties down on the Salerno plains.

The winding mountain roads across the backbone of Italy would however create a fantastic journey for their small group, passing through quaint villages that Ray swore portrayed an aspect of teetering at any moment towards the valley floor below.

Eventually everyone cheered as they rolled into the town of Gioia del

Colle, and onto the adjoining airfield liberally littered with Italian warplanes.

Tents ranged in neat rows through striking olive groves would serve as their billets and it wasn't long before by fair means or foul they'd won themselves a large, and Ray does mean *large*, at least a fifty or sixty-gallon barrel of vermouth, the sweet variety, which after a pow-wow everyone decreed would remain unopened until Christmas. Who got there first, I do not know, but Len's date for arrival at Gioia del Colle shows the 18th October 1943.

Pilots too were preoccupied with booze, with activities taking a back seat as far as war was concerned; Len implied their top priority was to outdo the other squadrons by fixing up a damn good mess. They were successful of course, making 152 the venue for all major 'pissies'. That plus bags of time for having a good look round Italy.

The first thing that struck Len was how pretty the girls were. Always one for the ladies, my brother from the age of seventeen cavorted with the fair sex. Athletic and a good dancer, he never went short of the right company, and now he sported the typical RAF moustache, one wouldn't be stretching the truth too far to say he was akin to an Errol Flynn or David Niven. On top of all this, as if that wasn't enough, his humour was boundless, he could draw exceedingly well, and he gave a squelching imitation of Donald Duck that would invariably have everybody in his company doubled over in stitches.

'Italy,' he wrote, 'even under war, is a dream of a place, by jimminy I'm a good mind to stop here and get married.'

When I first met Ray in 1998, I only had to mention Donald Duck, and the images in his mind came flooding back. 'How,' he uttered, 'could I ever have forgotten that?'

Adventure was constantly uppermost in everyone's mind, with little flying and a lovely country; it was only natural to make the most of one's opportunities.

Len's diary continues:

Having this time off one wanted to get out and see things, on one such day three of us went hitch hiking to a castle way up on a hill. Coming back I got fed up with walking so seeing an empty van in front took a peep round it, finding out that it was not owned by A. M. G. so jumping in starting it, it sounded ok. I then decided to take it so telling the boys to jump on went off down the road being chased by a couple of Ities so stepping on it and trying to get round a convoy

I went down a bomb hole in the middle of the road, no damage was done so off we went leaving the Italians on the other side of the hole.

Word came through we were moving again so packing our bags we went down to Gioia south of the bomb line this was to us a rest but none of us agreed with this. This place is in-between Taranto and Bari. Bari being the best place to go to a wizard place trams running and one can get food, the trouble was getting there so once a week the Sqd got the day off bagged a three tonner and off to Bari for a major pissy. Coming back from one of these do's we collided with an ambulance being way out in the middle of the road with full headlamps we neatly collected this swinging us into a wall smashing this down finishing up after knocking a tree down piled all in one corner of the lorry, I of course being underneath the lot. No one was hurt which was a good and splendid thing. The C/O wet crook at this but after an enquiry it came off in our favour.

While at Gioia, Ray remembers one of the RAF's lesser known (but most successful) aces dropping in to visit 152 – a certain Wing Commander (later Group Captain) P H 'Piet' Hugo, referred to as 'Dutch' (he was actually South African). His Spitfire Mk IX had been modified to take a 500 lb bomb on hooks where the belly tank usually went. As a professional in Spit bombers, Ray cast an inquisitive eye over this latest innovation.

When he and the boys eventually trekked off to Gioia del Colle one of the niceties they discovered was a very comprehensive hairdressing salon. One can imagine the look on the prestigious owner's face when these scruffy-haired British types honoured his premises. 'We asked for the lot,' grins Ray. 'Haircuts, shampoos, shaves, hot towels, and each time an erk sat in his chair he would mumble something in Italian as he shook his head in disgust.' But at least they looked and smelt a bit better than usual; sufficient, they felt, to enable each to pay a visit to the lovely city of Bari.

Four episodes affected Len's life about this period.

The crossed sword and scabbard which they hung in pride of place amidst the trophies in the squadron's mess that once belonged to Salerno's Chief of Police, was an item of war that nobody seemed to know how Smithy had won!

The second episode was a chance meeting that occurred whilst supping in a bar back in Serretella with an Italian pilot from the same Regia squadron they had bumped into when flying from Malta. During a conversation in mutual French between him and one of Smithy's pals determined that it had been he, Smithy, who had shot down their C/O. The meeting blossomed into friendship, with Len later writing in English and the Italian in French, to make for easier translation.

Thirdly, there was Len's rise, as Ray would say, to the exalted rank of Flight Sergeant, despite pleas to London from his superiors to win him a commission.

Writing to our sister Cecilia, he said, 'It's worth a Shilling a day Cissy, minus of course two Shillings and Sixpence a week income tax. I'm sorry but it doesn't look as though Air Min in London are ever going to forget my Flagpole do.'

Finally a flight to remember. Sitting at dispersal was a flight of special all-blue Spitfires. These kites had been stripped of their armour plate and machine-guns, giving them a good rate of climb. Bruce Ingram, the C/O, had selected ten of his best pilots to take turns in standing by to intercept high-flying aircraft, having to look out for vapour trails or be prepared for a sudden scramble. All ten were itching to have a go, but unfortunately or otherwise only on one occasion did anything untoward show up, and guess who was in the driving seat. Yes! Smithy!

He scooted up to 13,000 feet to discover they were our lads anyway. Excited he wrote, 'It did give me a chance to fly one of these special all blue jobs, terrific rate of climb and speed, the last word in Spitfires.'

Everybody realised they had been sent to this safe back area for a reason, they now stood two to three hundred miles from Naples and were equipped with the latest Mark IX Spits: just what was afoot? Ideas began to formulate like olives falling from a tree.

One of the most popular was an invasion through the Balkans or even Turkey, both scenarios put forward as the best way to link up with the Russians. Other explanations always leant towards a European direction as the obvious choice. Nothing of course could have been further from the truth.

A decidedly unpopular type, in the form of Ray's and the rest of the lads' Adjutant, approached them one day wagging a knowing finger and grinning like a Cheshire Cat. 'I know where you're going,' he tittered. 'You're going to Burma, and I'm not going with you!'

Types stood aghast, unbelieving, then it was their turn, letting him know just how disliked he was. They were thrilled, they choroused, at the second part of his message.

Things were going to happen fast, and the first priority was to make the most of that barrel of vermouth. Christmas was now definitely out, so a night of debauchery was selected. Ray remembers starting his second pint, but after that things got kinda hazy. All that he is sure of is that for years afterwards he couldn't look a glass of vermouth in the mouth without suffering severe heartburn.

Two squadrons were going, the other being No. 81. At least pilots were given the choice. Bruce came round to give them the gen, offering his pilots the chance to step away from this next move if they so wished. Not a man declined, so that was it, the die had been cast.

'We must operate over Burma by the first of December,' wrote Len, 'where if the Japs don't get us the jungle will!'

They all left in mid-November, gazing over the side of the SS *Talma* as she slid out of Taranto Harbour, their first stop Alexandria in Egypt. Len was wishing it were the English Channel, and I guess so was everyone else, but they were going even further away from home. Exciting as it may be in those days the thought could also be daunting.

1943- Tunisia - Len's Log

SINGLE-ENGINE AIRCRAFT				MULTI-ENGINE AIRCRAFT						PASS-ENGER	INSTR./CLOUD FLYING (Incl. in cols. (1) to (10).)	
DAY		NIGHT			DAY			NIGHT				
DUAL	PILOT	DUAL	PILOT	DUAL	1ST PILOT	2ND PILOT	DUAL	1ST PILOT	2ND PILOT		DUAL	PILOT
(1)	(2)	(3)	(4)	(5)	(6)	(7)	(8)	(9)	(10)	(11)	(12)	(13)
63·35	269·15	3·55	16·20	8·45						2·10	18·10	12·45
	1·40											
	1·00			(SOYDS MISS) MACHINE GUN & CANNON ON THREE JERRIES								
	1·20											
	·45											
	·50											
	·40											
	1·20			HEAVIEST FLAK EVER SEEN VERY SHAKY SHOT UP GUN HUT								
	1·10			LIGHT FLAK SIX JERRIES 10'000 ABOVE								
	1·30			LIGHT HEAVY FLAK ACURATE BUT MISSED								
	1·40											
	1·20			SLIGHT FLAK HURRICANES BOMBED AIRODROME								
	·50											
	·45			BOMBING TANKS NEAR MEDJEZ SLIGHT FLAK ALL ON TARGET								
	·50			SHOT DOWN IN FLAMMES 109G THAT JUMPED 1/ST SPARE								
	·55			HIT BY FLAK IN OIL TANK LANDED O·K·								
	1·35											
	1·25											
	1·25			JUMPED BY 109s DAMAGED ONE BIG DOG FIGHT								
	1·00											
	1·20											
	1·30											
	1·05											
	·40											
63·35	295·50	3·55	16·30	8·45						2·10	18·10	12·45
(1)	(2)	(3)	(4)	(5)	(6)	(7)	(8)	(9)	(10)	(11)	(12)	(13)

From April 10th to 27th
Len's April log declares one Messerschmitt 109g destroyed and one damaged.

Message on bombs reads
'This is it from Millie, Mum & Dad'

Len's caption reads
'My Kite just been cleaned'

Jeep full of A riggers

Stan shooting a line!!

1943 - Paddington Strip – Souk-el-Khemis – Tunisia

SINGLE-ENGINE AIRCRAFT				MULTI-ENGINE AIRCRAFT						PASS-ENGER	INSTR./CLOUD FLYING [Incl. in cols. (1) to (10)]	
DAY		NIGHT		DAY			NIGHT					
DUAL	PILOT	DUAL	PILOT	DUAL	1st PILOT	2ND PILOT	DUAL	1st PILOT	2ND PILOT		DUAL	PILOT
(1)	(2)	(3)	(4)	(5)	(6)	(7)	(8)	(9)	(10)	(11)	(12)	(13)
63·35	295·50	3·55	16·20	8·45						2·40	18·10	12·45
	·55				BOMBED ROAD	MACHINE GUN & CANNON FIRST HOUSE						
	·45		SEC LEO		BOMBED ROAD	DIRECT HIT ON TRANSPORT (WHOSE I DON'T KNOW)						
	1·10				BOMBED WADDIE HELD BY ENEMY TROOPS							
	1·00				DIRECT HITS WIPING OUT HUN HEADQUARTERS							
	1·25				TWO DIRECT HITS SLIGHT FLAK							
	31·40											
	292·05		10·10									
	50·00											
	1·20				SLIGHT FLAK							
	1·05		SEC LEO		SLIGHT FLAK							
	1·20				SMANY DO DIRS OF LIGHT FLAK SPIRE BLEED OUT "ARMSTRONG FORCE LANDED							
	1·00				HITS WHERE TANKS SHOULD HAVE BEEN LIGHT FLAK							
	1·10		SEC LEO		DIRECT HIT IN BETWEEN TRUCKS							
	1·10				JUMPED 109G SAW HITS BLACK SMOKE COMING FROM IT (PROBABLE)							
	1·05				DIVE BOMBED TRUCKS ALSO BELT THEM UP WITH CANNON SHELLS							
	1·20				DVE BOMBED TOWN HEADQUARTS HITS IN GERMAN PLANE BIG FIRE STARTED PLT. 323							
	1·10				TURNED BACK WITH BOMBS BAD WEATHER BAGS OF FLAK HIT ON ...							
	1·30				DIRECT HIT ON SHIP NO FLAK GROUND STRAFFED BARGES							
	1·35				DIRECT HIT ON FW 190 SET IT ON FIRE GROUND STRAFFED GROUND							
	1·40				DIRECT HIT ON ROAD STAFF CAR RAN INTO IT HAD TO FORCE LAND AT MEDJEZ THROUGH GLYCOL LEAK ENGINE AT HALF OFF							
63·35	316·90	3·55	16·20	8·45						2·40	18·10	12·45
(1)	(2)	(3)	(4)	(5)	(6)	(7)	(8)	(9)	(10)	(11)	(12)	(13)

From April 27 to May 9th
Len's log describes bombing runs and probable 109g

"THE"

Volume 1.   "PADDINGTON POST"   Number 18.

8000000000000000000

Saturday May 8th 1943

1 5 2   G I V E   H U N   N O   R E S T

AIRFIELDS BOMBED AS PLANES TAKE OFF

==

2 Me 109's Shot Down

+++

Today our airforces continued to harry the Hun as driven into the most North Easterly corner of Tunisia he fought his last fight of the North African campaign.

It was another splendid day for 152 Squadron, who carried their bombs to the most Easterly aerodromes and not only dropped them among dispersed aircraft but chased and shot down two Me 109's which had just taken off.

One of these was shared by F/Lt Baynham and F/O Tooth. They saw him circling the airfield and diving upon him chased him across country firing in turn until he crash landed at high speed at the foot of the hills West of Kelibia.

The other was chased out to sea by Sgt Glover, who scored hits on the cockpit hood probably wounding the pilot for the last he saw of the aircraft was as it rolled slowly on its back only ten feet above the sea. He was unable to see it go in for at that moment he was himself attacked by the Hun's number two and by the time he had driven him off there was nothing to be seen of the first aircraft.

The Squadron also scored a direct hit on a ship which was in the act of embarking troops and shot up Siebel Ferries and men on the beach near Lake Porto-Farina.

++++

RETREAT BECOMES ROUT

===

Hun Cornered in Peninsular

++++

After their break through yesterday our troops swept all before them today. The Hun this evening had been pushed into the Cap Bon Peninsular where he was constantly harried by bombers and ground straffing aircraft.

Pont du Fahs, for so long a thorn in the side of the Allies, fell this morning almost without opposition to the French troops who fought so extremely gallantly in this theatre despite inferior equipment.

There is now no doubt about it the retreat has become a rout Dunkirk is about to be avenged.

++++++

STOP PRESS

More Fun for 152!

***

There was more fun in store for 152 when they made their third visit of the day over the Hun lines this evening. On Menzel Temime airfield they found at least a dozen Ju 52's on the ground as well as several single engined aircraft.

Of these they left at least 4 in flames and riddled several more with canon and bomb splinters. The C.O. got two of the flamers, Sgt Smith got a direct hit with a bomb on a FW 190 and altogether it was a first class show.
Smithy gets a mention !!

1943 - Len's Log - Malta

SINGLE-ENGINE AIRCRAFT				MULTI-ENGINE AIRCRAFT						PASS-ENGER	INSTR/CLOUD FLYING [incl. in cols. (1) to (10)]	
DAY		NIGHT		DAY			NIGHT					
DUAL	PILOT	DUAL	PILOT	DUAL	1ST PILOT	2ND PILOT	DUAL	1ST PILOT	2ND PILOT		DUAL	PILOT
(1)	(2)	(3)	(4)	(5)	(6)	(7)	(8)	(9)	(10)	(11)	(12)	(13)
63·35	326·40	3·55	16·20	8·45						2·10	18·10	12·45
	·50											
	1·55			MACHI 202 HALF ROLLED NO HOPE OF CLOSING SGT ARMSTRONG BALED OUT								
				OVER SEA WAS PICKED UP								
	1·00											
	·40		1·10	A SIGHT WORTH SEEING FOR INVASION OF SICILY								
	1·35			COVERING TROOPS LANDING No FIGHTERS OR ENEMY BOMBERS SEEN								
	1·35			FIRED AT BY OWN GUNS.								
	1·20			190S BOMBED BEACH No HOPE OF CATCHING ACK ACK BIT NEAR								
			1·30	UNEVENTFULL EXCEPT FOR RED HOT TRACES VERY PRETTY BUT								
	1·40											
	·40		1·15	SAW TWO A/C COMING UP BEHIND CHASED BUT LOST IN DARKNESS								
	1·55			SAW 5 JERRY KITES CHASED TO FAR TO INTERSEPT								
	2·10			KITTYHAWKS BOMBED CATANIA LANDED WITH 4 GALLONS.								
	2·00											
	1·00											
	1·55											
	1·55			12 REGG 2000 ONE BOMBED CONVOY No HITS SHOT DOWN 1½ THE OTHER								
				1½ TOO F/O KINGSFORD, F/O JONES GOT 3 IN ALL PATROL BIGGER 6								
	1·30			ENGINE DUFF TURNED BACK								
	2·00			A BIT TOO FAR FOR MY LIKING								
64·35	360·40	3·55	20·30	8·45						2·10	19·10	12·45
(1)	(2)	(3)	(4)	(5)	(6)	(7)	(8)	(9)	(10)	(11)	(12)	(13)

From July 5th-20th
Len's log shows destroyed one Reggio 2000 and damaged another

Len draws his own destiny
1943. Len draws himself in the cockpit

June 1943 - The Malta Mob

Len's log depicts the Malta pilots of 152. Len is back row second from right.

1943. Lentini

Five Star living for 152

Still in Sicily
Hello Mum! Wish you were here!!

1943 - Len's Log from Lentini, Sicily

SINGLE-ENGINE AIRCRAFT							INSTR/CLOUD FLYING (incl. in cols. (1) to (10))	
DAY		NIGHT		DUAL				
DUAL	PILOT	DUAL	PILOT	DUAL			DUAL	PILOT
(1)	(2)	(3)	(4)	(5)			(12)	(13)
65.35	360.40	3.55	20.30	8.45			18.10	12.45
	1.00							
	1.40				REG MARSHALL WAS SHOT DOWN BY 109 BELIEVED KILLED			
	1.30				SHOT DOWN 109 WHO JUMPED US LED US INTO FLAK BUT SHAKY			
	.15							
	1.30							
	1.30				QUITE A BIT OF FLAK NOTHING SEEN			
	1.30				NOTHING SEEN IN THE WAY OF JERRYS, JUMPED SPITS			
	1.30				NO FLAPS			
	35:35	4:10						
	316.35							
	122:00							
			4.10		O.C. 152 Sqn			
	1.40							
	1.10							
	1.15							
	1.45				KEPT COVER FOR WALRUS PICKING UP PILOT IN SEA OFF 'CATANIA'			
	1.45				LAST PATROL WAS B.AGS OF ACCURATE FLAK 'Roy' HIT			
	1.00				NEARLY SHOT DOWN 'MUSTANGS' ANOTHER FRACTION OF A SECOND AND			
	1.05							
	.15							
	1.30							
65.35	382.40	3.55	20.30	8.45		2.10	18.10	12.45
(1)	(2)	(3)	(4)	(5)	(6)	(7)	(8)	(9)	(10)	(11)	(12)	(13)

F/O. R. A. Marshall, of Auckland, previously missing, now presumed dead.

From July 21st to August 12th.
Len's log depicts destruction of one Messerschmitt 109 and Loss of F/O H A Marshall

Italy - September 1943

Salerno Chief of Police, 2nd from right displaying sword won by Len

Sgts mess, Asa, Italy
Sword looks much better there!

1943 - Invasion of Italy

SINGLE-ENGINE AIRCRAFT						PASS-ENGER	INSTR./CLOUD FLYING (Incl. in cols. (1) to (10))	
DAY		NIGHT		DUAL				
DUAL	PILOT	DUAL	PILOT	DUAL			DUAL	PILOT
(1)	(2)	(3)	(4)	(5)		(11)	(12)	(13)
63.35	399.45	3.55	20.30	8.45		2.10	18.10	12.45
	.35							
	1.10			CHASED TWO A/C NO JOY				
	.30							
	2.55			90 GALLON TANKS TWO HOURS SPENT OVER WATER				
	2.35			HUNDREDS OF SMALL BOATS AMAZING SIGHT				
	2.50			NO ENEMY AIRCRAFT SEEN				
	3.10			CHASED TWO 190s NO JOY				
	2.30							
	2.25			CHASED 109 NO LUCK (A GOOD DAY)				
	2.20							
	2.40			BAGS OF SHELLING OUR TROOPS				
	2.00			CAME BACK WITH A/C ENGINE U/S GO GOT 109 DAMAGED				
	1.45			LANDED ON ITALY NORTH SIDE OF BATTLE LINE NAVY SHELLING ONE END				
				OF RUNWAY AND ARMY THE OTHER LANDING STRIP ONLY 700yds LONG				
				NEARLY WENT DOWN PITCH ALSO BALLOONS IN AREA				
	1.15			SAW BIG TANK BATTLE GOING ON				
	1.30			SHOT DOWN FW190 TRYING TO DIVE BOMB SHIPS SPEED 940mph				
	1.35			QUITE A BIT OF ACTIVITY ACK ACK ALL ROUND ENGINE WENT U/S				
	1.35			5 FW 190s TRIED TO BOMB SHIPS CHASED THEM HOME WITH BOMBS				
				STILL ON, TOOK AVPOF GOT DAMAGED 109 GOT ONE DESTROYED 190 ONE SHOT				
	1.40							
	1.40							
63.35	436.15	3.55	20.30	8.45		2.10	18.10	12.45
(1)	(2)	(3)	(4)	(5)	(6) (7) (8) (9) (10)	(11)	(12)	(13)

From September 6th to 22nd
Len's log shows destruction of one F W 190 and damage to another

Gioia Del Colle, Italy October 1943

Len records (Len second from left back row)
'I'm a bit tiffy here, also the rest when this was taken. We sort of painted the town red,
getting Janker the next day. Still it was worth it!!'

Port of Taranto, October 1943

INDIA–BURMA

1943–45

First omens were not good. Before a second ship, loaded with 152 technical support equipment, could leave port, the bombers came, sending it and sixteen other ships to the bottom. They included an American supply ship, the *John Harvey*, which was secretly carrying mustard gas bombs; the resulting casualties in the city of Bari were very high and spread over a long period, partly because rescuers were not aware that they were dealing with poison gas. (The incident was immediately hushed up on the orders of Churchill and other Allied leaders.)

Happily 152's complement of personnel did arrive safely at Alexandria, although it would appear ground staff had been separated from aircrew. Ray expressed no knowledge of their presence, but Len's records confirm that the SS *Talma* had indeed been his and the rest of the flying fraternity's transport, travelling very slowly and taking about six days to cover the zigzagging journeys.

The separation continued at Alexandria, with ground crews shunted to desert transit camps just outside town, and pilots finding themselves bundled into trucks before being whisked through the streets of Alex, heading towards Cairo and beyond to another tented area pitched in sand.

Two sights cheered Smithy on the way, an unusually shy American nurse dodging behind vehicles trying to avoid 152's leering swashbucklers as they sped through Alex, and arriving in darkness to Cairo's wondrous illuminations. It was the first completely lit-up city he had seen since sailing from Canada after winning his wings under the Empire Training Scheme at Moosejaw some three years earlier.

Being so close to Alex gave some of the lads, including Ray, time for a fleeting visit. Among the motley crew was a fellow called Guy Cartledge, known as 'Three O', a tag imposed because of his name, a .303 round being the standard *cartridge* of the time. Actually Guy was a pretty inoffensive type, so when accosted by a local Arab youngster wishing to know the importance or otherwise of a half-crown piece, Guy was at pains to oblige the urchin and was therefore somewhat surprised when the lad said he didn't want it, and would Guy give him a few piastres for it.

Never one to look a gift horse in the mouth, straightaway Guy fumbled for his wallet when, quick as a flash the little horror's number two rushed past, disappearing at a rate of knots, leaving poor 'Three O' staring at his empty hand.

That episode stayed with 152 for quite a while.

To give some indication of the light-fingered activities experienced by the services in that part of the world, Ray explains that strict instructions had been issued, that all pay-books must be secured to the person by passing a piece of string through a hole pierced in the book before entering the inside of the tunic and finishing up round the neck. For obvious reasons, pay-books were very much coveted by the enemy and could command much in the way of piastres.

Port Tewfik on the Bitter Lakes heralded 152 ground staff's next destination, leaving Alexandria after only two or three days to squeeze aboard lighters for the short hop to the SS *Strathmore*, now standing out in deeper water to take them and a load of pale-faced fresh-from-Blighty troops to the delights of Burma.

To these chaps Ray and his cohorts must have looked a rough lot, having been through three seaborne invasions, plus their recent journey aboard railway cattle trucks sitting on just their battle packs wasn't helping the image either. God! What a right load of brigands. At least that's how Ray felt!!

Nosing alongside the *Strathmore* each and everyone felt more than justified in sounding off a line shoot, a feeling amply exemplified when one wag amongst them yelled, 'Never mind the ruddy gangplank mate, just sling us some rope!'

Never in his wildest dreams did Ray imagine from that moment and for the next two years that they would be involved in halting the rampant Jap, now on the threshold of India, and push him back through Burma, from the far north to the distant south.

So they sailed from Port Tewfik, down the Red Sea, past Aden, and on to Bombay in that November 1943, leaving the pilots to journey to a place called Helwan and collect new Spitfire Mk VIIIs, 'the prettiest Spitfire ever built', and after flying them to Cairo West Aerodrome, take them in thirteen hops to the far side of India. Len said they were making history. First to Raffa, then a spot in the Iraqi desert near the pipeline called H3, from there to Habbaniya, and on to Shaibah, then the island of Bahrain, from there to Sharjah, and Jawani, on to Maripur, from here to Jodhpur, Delhi, Allahabad, Gaya, and finally Baigachi.

Unlike their ground crew, pilots had been able to visit the delights of Cairo a few times, for their stay had lasted ten days. Similar to Guy, Len also experienced a spot of bother, writing of a cabaret full of scantily clad dancing girls, 'It was a tough place, Turner and myself ending up trying to wreck the joint, we had good reason too!'

Journeying to Helwan to collect their new Spits pilots were decidedly nervous for some hadn't flown for nearly two months, it was going to be a long and arduous flight assisted by thirty-gallon overload tanks. The sentiment was reflected by Ray when he described it as 'a true flight of endurance in the cramped confines of a Spitfire cockpit'.

Leaving Raffa in the then country of Palestine, now Israel (a country I found myself in as part of the Sixth Airborne Division during the troubles of 1945–6) they flew to H3. Here they would be refuelled from petrol cans drawn from buried bunkers in the sand. This place Len mentions as being stuck out in the middle of bugger all, at least 600 miles from the nearest native town. He asked one of the boys looking after them what he thought of the place, getting the reply, 'We have nice weather.' 'It makes one think,' Len went on:

Believe me there wasn't a tree to be seen, just one long unending stretch of Tarmac Road right across the Desert, the RAF Station is one of the best being like a small town in itself. We stopped the night here, I just sat on the side of the bed, and when I woke up found I still had all my clothes on, for I must have been so tired.

Len continued with his last diary entry, why he discontinued is unknown but I only had his log-book entries and letters home to help me beyond this point, and of course dear Ray's memoirs.

We are really making good time the cruising speed of these Spits is around 230 to 240 what we will do when stripped of our tanks in the wings and our overload tanks will make the Japs open their eyes. This trip by the way is the first time that Spitfires were flown along this route so we are making history. Our next nights stop was at Bahrain Island our huts were built of cane but inside was electric lights also fans. They dived for pearls here and got oil from the land. Final entry.

Leaving Bahrain on the 29th November Len suffered a cable fault connecting his overload tank, being forced to return to the Island and join up the following day with 81 Squadron covering the same journey as 152 and lead by Sqn Ldr Babe Whitamore.

The day following, the last day of November, saw them over-flying the Kirther Mountains to enter India, and Smithy just made it after collecting yet another glycol leak, but fortunately despite his overheated engine being able to glide down to their next stop, Maripur. Here for awhile, the pilots would rest and be re-equipped with tropical gear, not continuing their flight across India until the 14th December.

Meanwhile, disembarking at Bombay, 152's ground crews also enjoyed the prospect of new clothing, including the by now, well outdated pith helmet. A measure of attire quickly discarded when everybody scrambled to acquire a bush hat for themselves.

It was here Ray recalls a certain Flight Sergeant in charge of stores trying to relieve him of his battledress tunic and admonishing him for its disgraceful condition, forcing Ray to relate the tale of his near miss at Souk-el-Arba. The explanation and reference to a good luck charm led the Flight Sergeant to relent, and two years later on his return to Bombay, Ray still had it in his possession.

The three-day rail journey across India to Calcutta and thence Baigachi became something of an eye opener. November still enjoyed the dry season and could often be quite warm; consequently at every stop made they were immediately accosted by beggars and char-wallahs (tea sellers). They discovered that some of the larger stations en-route had several restaurants because of the varying religions, requiring a delay of at least half an hour each time to cater for all and sundry. Each beggar seemed to suffer from terrible deformities, sometimes legless, sometimes, armless, or be horribly distorted through leprosy. The awful truth dawned when it appeared that the greater the deformity, the greater the asset.

Other scenes absorbed included many of the stations acting as actual homes for whole families, giving the appearance of a village like community. Meals openly cooked on the platforms, side tracks utilised as toilets, and everyone crowding the communal drinking fountains to clean their teeth with one finger. At night they all slept in the waiting rooms, or on mats scattered along the platform, with the beggars grabbing any odd corner possible. To Ray at the time such sights were unimaginable.

As each village slowly passed their vision, they could see women busily patting something by passing it from hand to hand, later to be confirmed as cow dung, which they expertly attached to their house walls, later to be removed and used as fuel for their fires.

The second class carriage seating they endured did not aspire to any upholstery, but consisted only of wooden lath like planking, not dissimilar to a park bench. After three days of this, one was inclined to suffer from a permanent impression, but when journeys end did arrive; they found their living quarters at Baigachi, consisting of what were termed bamboo bashas, to be total luxury compared to anything previously encountered abroad. Even the surroundings were extremely pleasant.

Here everyone would spend Christmas 1943.

The squadron was not destined to account for many Japanese aircraft in the air over the next two years, due entirely to lack of opportunity, however they would lend great support to the Fourteenth Army, giving close combat sorties to assist advancing ground troops, especially so during the last twelve months of the war. Despite this lack of opportunity they were still lucky enough within a few days to show the Japanese what a Spitfire Mk VIII could do.

Arriving at Baigachi on the fifteenth and immediately acclimatising himself to the surrounding area it was not long before Len became scrambled to intercept reported enemy aircraft.

The date was the 26th December. After a Christmas Day gathering which proved very festive and enjoyable compared to the miserable time 152 had experienced the previous year just after the North African landings, it would be nice to round the good times off with a 'shot at the Nips' on Boxing Day. Unfortunately Smithy experienced no luck, failing to make visual contact. In a parallel scramble though, reported by Ray and corroborated by Len's log, F/O R E J MacDonald, and Flt Sgt R O Patterson did.

Birth of the Black Panthers

Most days, as Ray so succinctly puts it with his tongue firmly in cheek, the Japs had been in the habit of sending over a reconnaissance plane to the Calcutta area, presumably to check on what films, if any, were being shown at cinemas along the Charangi, before doing an about turn towards base and the joys of saki and raw fish. On Boxing Day however this ritual would be different.

It was at 07.40 hrs that radar picked up something, sending Purple Section from No. 615 Squadron on a scramble. No. 615 did not possess MkVIIIs, and in any event they did not make contact.

At 08.05, 152 were alerted informing them that a suspected recce plane was approaching the Chittagong area. This time having grabbed height as fast as they could MacDonald and Patterson, both from Australia, spotted a twin-engine 'Dinah' (Mitsubishi Ki-46) approaching them 500 feet below their ceiling of 23,000 feet at 09.00; it was down sun, about a mile away, slightly left, and closing.

Obviously the Nip had not seen the Spitfires as it continued on its northwesterly course. As it flew past, both Aussies turned to follow, with their indicated airspeed showing just 240 mph. At this point the Nip spied the Spits, quickly dropping his nose to increase speed with both followers doing likewise. It was then that MacDonald reported a white flak-like burst between him and the Jap, the missile obviously projected as it failed to lose height before exploding. (Later, after landing, Mac found two or three small holes and dents in the nose and wing of his aircraft.)

Both Aussies now went full out, swiftly gaining on the Dinah, who in reply pulled lots of G, entering a steep climb, leaving each Spit hanging on their props trying to get in a shot, MacDonald firing a burst before practically stalling, but seeing no hits.

Then the Dinah itself became forced to complete a stall turn, swinging down to the right, with this time Patterson closing fast, seeing hits around the port engine causing this to catch fire, with a large chunk of wing also breaking away. Instantly the enemy plane fell into a violent dive, getting steeper and steeper; prepared for such a manoeuvre it became Mac's turn once more, following the Jap as his indicator rose beyond 400 mph, managing to catch the Dinah with three more long bursts before easing back on the stick, his speed registering 460 mph. The Dinah's starboard engine began to flicker until finally it plummeted earthwards with both engines engulfed in flame and smoke.

Afterwards, reports indicated that it had indeed been a twin-engine Dinah, possibly of the Mk III variety.

Ray concludes: 'Thus it was that 152 Squadron became one of only three squadrons in the RAF to claim victory over all three enemy Axis aircraft, German, Italian and Japanese. The other two squadrons being numbers 30 and 81.'

One evening early in the New Year Ray decided it was time to give his kit bag a birthday, and the easiest way to accomplish this was to literally up-end the thing, allowing its accumulated contents to spread over the floor. What should tumble out last was none other than his long forgotten lemons, so quickly prising open the tin he was amazed to find they were still as green as the day he won them from Italy. This was his cue to wrap the lot, box and all, in some hessian and straightaway post them to mum.

In January 1946 when he finally returned home, the first thing his mum said was how lovely the lemons had been, having arrived in perfect condition and causing her homemade lemon curd to be the envy of the whole street. Don't forget – Britain during the war and even for some time after never saw such delights.

Quite close to Ray's clearout, January 5th to be exact, whilst Len was acting as a target stooge, another of 152's pilots would be lost, this time Sgt Charlie Cole. After acting strangely, Charlie's plane just plummeted to earth with Charlie slumped over the controls. Yet again the cause had all the hallmarks of oxygen failure.

Upon 152's arrival in India one thing that initially puzzled and even amused everyone, was the habit that the locals and old hands seem to have, particularly when caught in the open, of protecting their food. They would act quite furtively at times, hanging onto their plate with one hand whilst trying to cover the whole thing with the other.

This strange behaviour soon became understood however, when the first Kite Hawk swooped from the sky. This scavenger stood larger than the English Sparrow Hawk, and would think nothing of diving down and grabbing your complete meal by its talons if you so much as gave it half a chance.

Another aspect that affected newcomers quite badly was the shock of seeing for the first time the abject poverty of so many of the natives. Ray found it almost beyond belief. Calcutta's streets thronged with thousand upon thousands of people all living, working and dying in the same area. These were the so called untouchables, the lowest of the low in the Hindu caste system.

Towards the end of 1943 there had been a bad famine and our servicemen witnessed the many bodies strewn across the pavements of those who had died during the night from starvation.

It was fascinating to see most of the chores enacted in the streets. A huge length of smoldering rope hanging from most corners for all and sundry to light their cigarettes. A barber squatting in the gutter his customer squatting in front of him being shaved by a double-edged safety razor-blade, stuck in a piece of wood for a handle.

Villagers did fare a little better, each one had a small pond or tank, usually man-made, in which they could wash their clothes, and themselves, and wash their mouths out, but sometimes they caught fish from the same water, so perhaps it wasn't as bad as it appeared. Everyone quite believed it though when they were informed that the life span of the average Indian was twenty-three years. To cap it all India's sacred cow was free to roam the streets, feeding as they wished from shops and stalls alike.

Little air activity took place in January other than practice flights and the odd abortive scramble. On the 15th Len carried out an interception but they proved friendly.

Ray on the other hand found himself travelling by rail to Secunderabad, southern central India, in the state of our benefactor, Hyderabad. Here he would be indoctrinated into the ways of command, including drilling squads of other corporals, as well as receiving certain administrative instruction. Not forgetting several games of football, and once he dropped the line of being attached to the Hyderabad Squadron to all the civvies working for his Highness he couldn't go wrong. 'Treated me like a damn VIP,' he said.

Sleeping quarters prior to the war had been the Nizam's Summer Palace. Each room contained lovely beds, called charpoys, together with suspended and draped mosquito netting. Each morning they would grab the nets by their corners and squeeze tight, until their hands ran red with the blood of hundreds of bugs, due to them actually multiplying at night.

Successfully completing the course with a seventy percent mark, Ray realised his promotion to sergeant should now only be a formality, once the powers that be felt the time was right.

By this time Len had yet again been passed over for officer status, with his C/O Bruce Ingram requesting that the Air Mininistry in London bury the flagpole incident, at the same time recommending his now senior squadron

NCO for recognition for meritorious service, for his coolness, cheerfulness, and bravery, which had become an inspiration to both pilots and ground crew alike. A pilot who whilst in support of the First Army had destroyed four and half enemy aircraft in the air plus many ground targets.

By the 21st February 152 had moved again, this time to Double Mooring, nearer to Chittagong. Sometimes pilots would have to fly even closer to the front line to a place called Ramoo. Len describes the whole area as pretty grim, but let's follow Ray's comments.

Some of the boys went on detachment to a place called Ramoo further down the Arakan Front, on the Eastern Shore of the Bay of Bengal.

This was a particularly unpleasant part of the world, both climatically and as far as the countryside was concerned to say that the coastline in many parts was Mangrove Swamp will give you some idea of what I mean.

I went for a dip in the sea, which remained very shallow for hundreds of yards and quite murky.

There appeared to be swarms of minute crawly creatures not dissimilar to Crabs that had a tendency to nibble you all over but left no visible signs of their activities. After closer inspection I suddenly realised the sea was completely full of the little devils. Needless to say I beat a hasty retreat and never bothered them again.

... The Nip at this time were attacking heavily on this front in an attempt to break through and capture Calcutta, and with it would grab the rest of India. He perpetrated many atrocities in this area bayoneting the wounded occupants of an Army Hospital and shooting all the Doctors.

Throughout the rest of February and the whole of March, squadron duties would be taken up with the odd abortive scramble. Sometimes flying to Ramoo a hundred miles up country and returning before dark. Reconnaissance flights over the area of Akyab, air tests, and escort duties. These latter were performed on behalf of Lord Louis Mountbatten. Smithy did quite a few of these and one day would meet the Supremo.

Lieutenant General Stilwell's GHQ issued a bulletin on the 11th March stating that Sino-American forces were within sixty miles of the Mandalay-Myitkyina Railway, and that mopping up operations against the Japanese

Birth of the Black Panthers

Eighteenth Division had begun in which 2000 of the enemy had been killed. But by 26th May they were still fighting to take Myitkyina, every yard becoming a desperate struggle, with only half the town falling into Allied hands by June 1st.

All this was taking place 250 miles as the crow flies due east of Imphal and a lot further on the ground, about three or four times further as each track wound back and forth through dense jungle and rugged mountain terrain. The wily Jap was far from beaten yet!

On March 28th Len wrote home; we would not receive another letter until early June. To satisfy the curiosity of Ciss (our eldest sister) about his life and surroundings he writes:

I could tell you what this place is like in two words, but seeing you're a lady it goes like this.

First the country itself is nearly under water, making it very swampy, causing dense undergrowth and every kind of Tree.

To get through the jungle would take a week to walk ten miles, having to cut your way through every inch.

It frightens me when I look down on it. During the day it gets hot I should say very hot with a slight breeze. The Bamboo Huts we live in are good protection, having trellis work near the roof and floor which allows the breeze to blow through.

Around us we have a native village, a queer bunch, you never see their women, and when they get married, beat the drums for ten days outside the couple's Hut. Bit of a bind that!

We are constantly sweating and surrounded by Mosquito's and every variety of insect. We have to continually change our shirts, but somehow I seem to be immune from any bites being able to keep my sleeves rolled up.

They smother the legs of our Beds with a Tar type substance to outwit the creepy crawlies, and before jumping in the other night I had to chase four Frogs and one Tree Rat away. This latter is something like a Squirrel with a long bushy tail. But the Snakes are the worst.

All night long you hear the locals wailing to Allah or somebody.

He decides to close but before doing so proceeds to paint a picture of himself and his current existence. How sometimes the sheer boredom can be worse than the fighting or the weather!!

There's a thing, I wonder if you really know me!

I am currently sitting on my bed, Camp Bed, Blankets two, writing by the light of a candle.

Outside are two longish Huts made of Bamboo with straw roofing. One for meals, t'other for recreation, both are identical, having a long table with a bamboo seat either side.

These Huts are in a clearing of the jungle, and at this present moment there are noise's which give you the creeps, but also that little bit of excitement.

I'm sweating like a pig with the heat, and I haven't shaved for it's a waste of time and razor blades, I'm not the only one!

Each day we stand by for the wily Jap, getting in the odd scramble.

This is from dawn to dusk, coming back to sit at the table bearded and sweaty, looking at the same people on the other side, where we all go 'Boo!' and make faces at each other! Nothing else to do! then into the other hut, to do what! Nothing! We've done it all before. Darts! and a game of Dominoes, but this game has become dangerous.

Four people play and the others look on booing and cheering whoever they want to win, and of course the guy that loses gets mad, sometimes me!

That's the game they want me to play now, they are shouting across telling me to cut this off short, I'd better go!

It's also the 28th today so we'll have to celebrate, we celebrate every-time we remember the day and date! Funny life isn't it! But its damn good, makes a man of you!

At around this time F/O Norman Jones DFC, who'd been with Len over the Salerno beachhead in Spitfire IXs when Len got his FW 190, became promoted to Flight Lieutenant and would lead A Flight.

It was now April 1st and they had been briefed for a sweep over the Meiktila area, a strategic airfield and railroad complex for transporting Japanese goods of war up from Rangoon. Each plane bore the ninety-gallon drop tank beneath its belly. A Flight were 180 miles behind enemy lines with these extra tanks just about empty when Flt Lt Jones came over the R/T to inform everyone he could not switch fuel tanks and the Spit was running dry. At the last moment Jonesy put her on her back and fell out, with Smithy and the rest of A Flight watching him float towards the thickly carpeted jungle floor.

Len's Log notes the cryptic comment, 'There's a hope.'

There was indeed hope and Ray tells us that Norman walked back into camp some ten or twelve days later.

At Ray's eightieth birthday party where I met Flt Lt Norman Jones DFC, I asked him to recall this episode, for when writing of my brother's exploits I'd fictionalised his return as being rescued by a long range Indian patrol force. This, he assured me, was not far from the actual truth, for in essence after struggling through impenetrable jungle for two or more days he came across a river where on the opposite bank he saw a village.

Now Ray says that pilots were told that if finding themselves behind enemy lines they were if possible to make contact with the headman of a village, as invariably they were pro-Allies. Norman, on the other hand, told me that they had been warned to be careful of village tribes as some had been known to be headhunters. Despite this thought however, by this time Norman said he was so desperate he took a calculated chance, and fortunately was welcomed and taken care of.

One day he noticed one of the men looking a little different to others in the village and also clad in a khaki tunic with the letters PR on the lapels. 'Punjab Regiment?' enquired Norman, to which the guy nodded. After that it was all plain sailing with his latest discovery promising to get him back home.

Flt Lt Jones would not fly over enemy territory again. After his debriefing the RAF felt it would be too risky to allow their officer to be caught by the Japanese; they tended to treat that type of escape as espionage and he could very well be executed, so Norman found himself repatriated home, which turned out not to be such a bad April Fools Day disaster after all.

Not everyone could count on Lady Luck holding forth a helping hand though. With flying weather positively fearful and the terrain so bad, in most instances should misfortune strike, the whole plane and crew could be swallowed, lost without trace forever. Such a development happened just three days later, during another sweep over Meiktila, when Flt Sgt Berry was lost, his plane vanishing into the forest below.

Len wrote, 'Flt Sgt Berry spun in, out of cloud. There's no hope!'

Before the month expired F/O George King also suffered a malfunction of changeover from overload to main fuel tank, yet again in the Meiktila area. He stayed with his machine and managed to pancake. Len had him shown as killed; in fact the whole squadron were of the same opinion because George had disappeared from view. In actual fact he'd made contact with a native village, only this time as rotten luck would have it instead of being friendly the headman turned out to be pro-Japanese. As a consequence George found himself handed over to the Japanese, spending the remaining fifteen months of the war as guest of the Emperor in Rangoon jail.

Not discovering he had survived until 1991 Ray subsequently received a visit from George and his lady wife. He had been posted to 152 whilst they were in North Africa but had not caught up with them until Sicily so he'd obviously travelled around a bit. Before the war, as a boy George had been working for a store supplying goods to the cash and carry trade and after the war's end returned to eventually reach managing director status. Sadly George passed away in 1993.

In the early days of April Len did manage to join three scrambles, but each time no luck.

The day before losing Flt Sgt Berry he'd acted as escort to the Viceroy of India which turned out to be a bit of a bind when his Highness's plane flew too slowly for a Spit to keep station. Then on the 29th a ground strafe of Meiktila turned into a wizard show with a gun post destroyed and all aircraft safely returned.

Whilst in the Arakan Ray encountered something unusual which at the time struck a nerve but later made him giggle. Returning from an early stint at the strip one morning, he decided to detour in answer to the call of nature. To paint the picture, this abode consisted of bamboo poles plaited with banana leaves, thus granting a measure of privacy. A gap about eighteen inches from the ground upwards completed the structure, not in the least like your normal smallest room in the house, which they called an atapi, *atap* being the name given to the dry foliage used in the construction.

Calmly minding his own business Ray proceeded to embark upon his task, when from the corner of one eye he spied what can only be described as a slit eyed monster. In truth the six foot long apparition was actually a Monitor Lizard. Nothing to be unduly alarmed about of course, in fact the inquisitive creature was probably just as shocked spying Ray with trousers at half-mast as his nervous sitter was.

During the month of April three further events were to happen, firstly Len enjoyed a boozy twenty-fourth birthday on the 14th, then someone with whom he would strike up an affinity joined the squadron fresh from Blighty, namely Warrant Officer John Willoughby Vickers. At six feet one inch John stood some four and half inches taller than Smithy. Vicky and his family would one day meet with our own, and he would come to describe brother Len as 'very competitive with a great presence of mind'.

The third and most important event of April was two major offensives by Japanese forces at Imphal, this action being their final phase of a three-pronged attack across the half-mile wide Chindwin River. Each column consisting of one Division striking in a pincer movement west of Thaundut and Ukhrul had entered the State of Maripur on March 22nd thus threatening Kohima, bringing them by April 5th to within eight miles of Imphal, capital of Maripur and now able to cut our only overland route. The road to Kohima!

Ray records his memoir:

The squadron visited other strips throughout this period including Chittagong, Camilla, and Rumkahlong.

The Nips had gambled on a quick decisive result, in as much as they had attacked with minimum supplies, hoping to obtain what they required at the end of a successful campaign.

When they failed to reach their objective they were lost and the next attempt to penetrate India came at Imphal where they suddenly appeared from over the Chindwin and attempted to cut the road from Imphal to Dinapur and the railway to Calcutta.

The Imphal is a huge plain surrounded by 8,000 ft mountains with the main base of the Fourteenth Army on the central front further to the east of the Arakan and it was essential therefore that the line be held.

As these dire consequences dawned ferocious fighting escalated but it became too late as the enemy gradually closed the gap. Totally surrounded with enemy forces fast occupying all available high ground, four British divisions became trapped inside a plain forty-five miles long by twenty miles wide, giving Jap artillery looking straight down their barrels the prospect of a turkey shoot.

All unnecessary personnel would be immediately evacuated from the plain and hastily replaced with fighting units. It was also deemed prudent to bring in more fighter squadrons for defence and escort duties, and to this end on May 14th 152 found ourselves transferred at short notice to a strip inside 'the Box' at the southern tip of Imphal, called Palel.

Only very essential ground crews must be flown in by Dakota, giving me a chance to look down on the thickly covered jungle and for the very first time appreciate that any descent towards it meant disappearing for months if not forever. The whole of the plain had become one vast encampment, only able bodied people could be catered for, not one unnecessary mouth able to be entertained, meaning the plane you flew in also had to be offloaded by you too. A situation that I quickly discovered as we sweated to drag personal gear and maintenance equipment expeditiously from the briefly parked Dak at Imphal's main runway and hastily head for Palel and the servicing of 152's Spits.

As far as I was concerned the whole escapade seemed decidedly dodgy. At night after operations ceased we would retire to our domestic quarters, a tented area on the hillside surrounded by barbed wire. This abode completely boxed in by the wire was somewhere that you left at your peril, there were no courtesies here of 'Halt who goes there'. Anybody found beyond this designated perimeter was enemy, full stop.

Food rations became minimal, consisting mainly of one tin of corned beef between two each day, plus a few hard biscuits, bits of which we would nibble as we squatted apprehensively after dark round the odd hurricane lamp.

Every night the Japanese sent over raiding parties, creeping across the Burmese border only a short distance to the south, striking hard to inflict as much damage as possible before swiftly vanishing again from whence they'd come.

Len's first sortie from Palel took place on the day they arrived searching for reported bandits but failing to make contact. After that the weather closed in. At this time of year thunderheads could be particularly spiteful, you never flew through them unless you wanted to experience the contortions of a fly in a washing machine, even so 300 Dakotas and converted Mitchell bombers would be needed to run the gauntlet every day to keep the garrison inside what came to be known as the 'Imphal Box' supplied.

Palel was about thirty miles south of the main Imphal runway, which itself boasted a bizarre story, for when the American engineers were issued instructions as to its construction, the required length designated had been denoted in feet. The USA surveyors however only ever dealt in yards, leaving the finished enterprise stretching 4000 yards instead of feet, almost two and a half miles long. The resultant mistake proved absolutely vital for each time the enemy shelled one end, everybody took off and landed at t'other.

Words running through Len's log describe the difficulties of trying to keep supplying Dakotas in view, sometimes because of their straggled formations and quite often because of low cloud. Jap fighters did not seem to be too much in evidence, no doubt because of the heavy escorts provided but towards the end of June he did give chase to two Bead fighters[6] following them down to tree level before they managed to elude him.

During the middle of this campaign Ray finally succumbed to malaria. Strangely enough he thought himself lucky, for not long after orders arrived stating that due to the issue of Mepacrine, the malaria suppressant, anyone contracting the illness could be construed as having a self-inflicted injury, and thereby subject to disciplinary action.

It had been estimated at this time that malaria accounted for approximately a twenty-five percent wastage within the Fourteenth Army, and anyone catching it could end up in an Indian hospital for at least three weeks. However because of the dire situation, Ray could count on only three or four days in a casualty clearing station, where he would receive a strong dosage of quinine. This apparently solved the malaria problem but invoked violent sickness and virtual deafness.

In the end they realised there was nothing further they could do so promptly dispatched him back to the squadron, where 152's MO, taking one look at him, diagnosed yellow jaundice. Treatment for this malady required an essential fat free diet, of which bully beef and biscuits could not be a part, leaving evacuation by air from beyond the trouble spot the only alternative.

Life became somewhat hazy at this point as Ray struggled to remain in charge of his faculties. Reeling from a sense of groggy and fainting symptoms a two to three day journey aboard a hospital train seemed to gel, what he definitely recalled was a distinct lack of fat free food. A typical breakfast consisting of soya linked sausages and streaky bacon.

At an interim hospital after the exhausting train journey the staple diet still lacked any fat free food, and not until his final destination who's whereabouts remains a complete mystery to this day, did any appropriate cuisine rise to the surface. He did remember his surroundings fairly well,

---

6 Len's log reads: 'June 27 Escort Hurri bombers Kalewa – Chased two a/c down to deck (no luck Bead Fighters).' What kind of aircraft a 'Bead' fighter might be is not known.

being housed in typical bamboo basha type dwellings with the usual flaps acting as windows, and about forty other types suffering yellow skins and eyes, referred to each morning by Matron as her yellow canaries.

Subsequently declared fit enough for sick leave they actually asked him where he would like to go, unable to say home unfortunately, he decided on the next best thing, a name he'd once heard sounding like 'Nine-e-Tel', situated among the foothills of the Himalayas.

He guesses they didn't argue for he found himself journeying through India yet again, having to change trains at Lucknow in north central India to reach this holiday destination.

The hotel definitely sported five star status perched predominantly on the edge of a fairly extensive lake surrounded by forested hills. Top quality eating appeared to be the order of the day with a Bearer bringing tea covered with fresh lime leaves each morning whilst he lay in bed, and even polishing his shoes just for good measure. Altogether definitely the life of a wealthy Sahib he thought.

Quite a few private schools catering for white children dominated the area with one or two local bazaars thrown in. It was in one of these that Ray managed to get a signet ring, given in 1941, duly engraved. A piece of memorabilia still treasured to this day.

Ten days later duty again beckoned with still no-one asking for any money for all these unheard-of services, thank goodness, and for the next two days he doesn't remember seeing another service type as slowly he journeyed via Lucknow back to Calcutta. From this point eastwards though each carriage teemed with little else but uniforms.

Fighting on the road from Imphal to Dinapur had been particularly fierce and bloody, none more so than at Kohima, a hill station midway.

Here the famous battle of the tennis court alongside the governor's house had ensued for several weeks. It seems hard to envisage such a close viscous encounter with the Japanese literally on one baseline and British troops on the other. Each night both sides would send out raiding parties, with bayonets fixed, one can only imagine the terrible consequences of these encounters in pitch darkness.

Relief came on the 22nd June when an Allied column, breaking through from Imphal, met a corresponding force driving down the road from Dinapur at Milestone 109. A position just north of Imphal and the encircled plain.

Throughout this whole catastrophic period it would have been impossible for the British garrison to have survived the onslaught, had it not been for the thousands upon thousands of supply drops made by hundreds of Dakotas supplemented by the converted Mitchell bombers. A truly remarkable feat of endurance performed over some of the world's worst territory and in weather conditions bordering on the ridiculous.

As it transpired the outcome enabled Ray to rejoin 152 by the reinstated land route of locomotive travel from Calcutta to Dinapur, and thence by gharri 'truck' over the mountains via Kohima to drop down into the Imphal valley. Roughly half-way between Calcutta and Dinapur you had to change trains, leaving one side of the river to journey some six hours by boat to reach the far side.

The crossing took place near the confluence of the Ganges and Brahmaputra rivers, but by far the most magnificent part of this journey was the winding climb over the mountains from Dinapur, with staggering outcrops rising hundreds of feet on one side, as you looked down into equally spectacular forested ravines on the other – then quite suddenly to enter what could only be described as Moonscape as one became confronted by the appalling spectacle of Kohima, or what was left of it! As far as one could see it seemed for miles as though all the trees had been chewed off about six feet from ground level.

Throughout the siege everything had been dropped by air – ammunition, food, even tarpaulins to catch the monsoon rain for no water supply existed. It had taken forty days of bloody fighting, with more than 4,000 Japanese dead, to win this battle, over ground of unimaginable topography. British losses had not been inconsequential either!

Quoting from official records: 'Armour and Infantry had advanced under smoke and fire screens of guns and mortars, dive bombers and fighters, whilst from the high ground camouflaged medium Artillery piled on their weight to the flail of fire which beat out a path down which XXXIII Corps marched to keep the date with IV Corps at Milestone 109.'

Kohima stood at the highest point of the journey with the trail now leading straight down into the Imphal Plain below. So treacherous was the road and so steep the ravines that it was not uncommon to sight the odd Indian driver squatting at the roadside, his vehicle embedded at the bottom of the chasm. Ray said the ride constituted a thrill a minute.

To journey through the surrounding jungle-covered mountains so dense and impenetrable as they were, it begged the question of just how inventive and resourceful the wily Jap must have been. How one wonders! did he ever manage to get his equipment and artillery into these impossible positions and thereby surround and cut off the British so effectively.

Below, the valley of Imphal held all the hallmarks of Shangri-La, the whole plain being extremely fertile and blessed by a temperate climate. With plenty of sunshine and enjoying its fair share of monsoon weather, everything edible grew in profuse abundance, there was even a huge lake full of every kind of wildfowl and fish, a venue which Ray experienced later in the year.

With his return and the threat of the Japanese encirclement removed so too did the remainder of the ground crew enjoy a reunion, meaning that the squadron could operate once more as a complete unit.

Life during these absences had been far from dull.

As soon as the road had been reopened 152 went over to an attacking role, with Len leading two sorties on the last day of the month and claiming twelve sampans destroyed and eleven trucks. Again during the first week of July the figures began to mount with eighteen trucks destroyed or severely damaged.

It was during this period that the C/O approached Ray.

'Corporal Johnson,' he queried, 'you saw Group Captain Hugo's Spit Nine in Italy with a 500 pound bomb fitted?'

'Certainly did,' acknowledged Ray, so straightaway Bruce asked if he could do the same for his Mk VIII machine. After scratching his head a little, Ray said he thought he could and would give it a try, but cheekily added, 'If it doesn't work you must promise not to come back and complain about it.'

Where else could a corporal speak to his C/O in such a manner, other than inside a fighter squadron during a fraught and difficult campaign?

The story goes that their Sergeant Fitter Armourer Joe O'Sullivan had been taken ill in Italy and been left behind when the squadron sailed for India, but lo and behold had suddenly materialised out of the blue at Palel. He of course had not seen Hugo's Spit so Ray filled him in on as many of the details as he could. Between them both the Sergeant and his Corporal managed to fabricate a simple framework using two inch mild steel angle removed from the local barbed wire defences. Incorporated with this they utilised the existing belly tank hooks and rear spigot together with the release mechanism from the tank and offered the whole lot up to Bruce's Spitfire.

By way of testing the strength of this home-made devise both the innovators clung on tight, five foot six inch Ray with his youthful eight stone, and his slightly bigger senior at a heftier nine stone. The two of them together totalling only a mere 238 pounds needing to bounce up and down to simulate a 500 pound bomb. Carrying out this exercise over and over they did eventually manage to get the thing to work without bending. Ray couldn't help wondering what the Ministry Experimental Establishments back home would have made of it all.

Now all they had to do was to scrounge some bomb rack fittings from the adjacent Hurribomber squadron and they were in business.

After carrying out a number of sorties with this arrangement the C/O was over the moon, having become the first Spitty squadron to drop 500 lb bombs. The beauty of it was that if you got into difficulties you could let the whole damn lot go, bomb and carrier, just like jettisoning the fuel tank.

Everyone thought highly of Bruce; he really was a great guy. Born in Dunedin, New Zealand on the 13th December 1921 he was actually eight months Smithy's junior. While his father rose to be Dunedin's Fire Chief, Bruce became a clerk before entering the RNZAF in July 1941. Winning his wings as a Sergeant Pilot he was shipped to the UK to join 66 Squadron, moving very quickly to 611 Squadron.

Receiving a commission in March 1942 he again became posted, this time to 486 Squadron, formed as New Zealand's second fighter squadron. However this was once more to be short-lived when he found himself sailing with 601 Squadron on the American aircraft carrier USS *Wasp*. From here the pilots took off for Malta on the 20th April 1942, more than a year before Len flew from the same Island.

Before they left Malta for Egypt in June, Bruce had been responsible for destroying one Junkers 88 and sharing in the destruction of two more. Flying and fighting over the Western Desert his score continued to rise, sharing a Bf 109 on the 14th July and shooting down another a week later. During the months of September and October he successfully destroyed two more and damaged a further three. On November 7th when 601 intercepted Stukas over Matruh, Bruce managed to shoot down one of the escorting 109s and share in the destruction of a further Junkers Ju 87. On the 8th December he scored his last victory in the Middle East by shooting down a Bf 109 over El Agheila.

By now Ingram had become a flight commander and been awarded the DFC. In the following August he was to take command of 152 at Lentini East in Sicily.

As John 'Vicky' Vickers took off from Palel on the 7th of July he suffered the misfortune of a burst tyre, but did manage to get the kite airborne. After completing ground strafes against the Japanese, Bruce radioed Vicky to stay aloft while he brought the rest of the squadron in. After all the boys were safely down, he then instructed Vicky to make certain his harness was really tight and come in for a wheels up landing to one side of the strip.

Holding her off till the last minute Vicky accomplished this task without performing any silly ground-loops, whereby Bruce quickly had him airborne again in another Spit to keep pilot confidence and ability on the top line. Just as when falling off a horse and remounting.

Come the afternoon of that very day when returning from a further ground attack, it became their C/O's turn to do a wheels up pancake, this time short of the strip, presumably due to fuel problems. Whilst I am sure Ingram would carry out the same safety measures he had only that morning exhorted one of his charges to make certain of, he nevertheless suffered a broken nose and lacerations to his face from contact with the Spit's gunsight. These injuries were neither serious or life threatening in themselves, and Bruce was happily removed to a field hospital at Imphal.

Sadly however tetanus and malaria quickly set in and two nurses were sent post haste from Headquarters to attend Bruce's sudden deterioration. Despite every effort afforded by these angels of mercy, Bruce the unbeaten fighter in the air was unable to see off these despicable intruders invading his body and succumbed only four days later on the 11th July 1944.

No. 152 were devastated. Ray wrote of this popular and respected officer admired by both ground and air crew alike. Len would act as one of the pall bearers to an honoured and treasured friend, and later wrote home to his number one girl, our eldest sister Cecilia (Ciss). Constrained by censorship he first bemoans the monsoons, making flying very difficult, he describes sitting on a hill overlooking a valley, with bags of clouds and rain all round.

Sister Elsie asks how we boys stick it! I often wonder myself! food is wicked, just one small piece of bully and two slices of bread. Think I've got used to the heat but everything you wear is damp or wet, and boots get clogged with mud.

We heard about the Second Front and we out here think the Air

Force as regards fighters should be doing better. Believe me, give any one of our boys the chance to fight over there he'd make their eyes open, even better with a Squadron.

To think, no jungle, and you can fly free without carrying great knives, food, guns, everything to keep a person going for two weeks, plus the defending part against the Jap.

It sounds so silly to us hearing about their deeds. Why! They can go to the flicks when finished patrol, and take out their best girl, while we ourselves are never mentioned!

The boys out here get killed in a way that would make them shudder.

Well I guess that's my bind over.

It was very true that during the start of the second front, and even before and after it, most of the media seemed to concentrate on the war in Europe, any news coverage of the far east usually centred around the engagements of USA forces. It could be very disheartening and at one time our forces fighting to recapture Burma were called the Forgotten Army.

With the taking of Rome in Italy and Russian advances of up to 250 miles inside three weeks, as well as the breakthrough in Normandy, it could be understood. But one journal after the war did say that the terrible campaign for Burma had been fought for well over a year under the worst possible conditions and against a ruthless and clever enemy. It had been not so much a battle with bullets and bombs as with sheer guts and the will to carry on in the face of all odds. A determination in which the Fourteenth Army and the RAF had excelled.

Len had also written that he had now been acting as deputy flight commander, able to lead a section into battle, something he'd always wanted to do. 'That's a Flight Lieutenant's job really, so if I do get commissioned that puts me on the right road.'

But he was counting the days to home: 'may only be eighteen months now, and when I do I shall have to bring my Sword for I have already carried the damn thing 8,000 miles and must get it home after that!'

Command of the squadron passed to Captain W H Hoffe DFC, B Flight's leader, immediately promoted to Major and becoming the first South African to command a Spitfire squadron.[7] Harry Hoffe was yet another well liked

---

7 Hoffe was a member of the South African Air Force, hence the non-RAF rank of Major.

officer, a gentleman I had the good fortune and honour to speak over the phone and correspond with in 1997. Harry, by then a long-retired architect, had been happily married to Pauline for just over fifty years, celebrating their golden wedding with their children and grandchildren, all twenty-one of them. Speaking of the war and his part in it, he could only dwell on how lucky he had been to survive compared to so many others. A Commonwealth citizen and a staunch supporter of Britain and all she then stood for.

Harry's takeover would herald a month of frenzied activity as 152 and surrounding squadrons harried the Jap from dawn to dusk throughout August. Constantly Len's log read like a Sweet Dish, as time after time he would enter, Rhubarb Chindwin, Rhubarb Chindwin, coupled with a few cryptic comments.

Strafed Motor Launches we claim two destroyed,three damaged.
Strafed three Sampans and destroyed Motor Launch.
Strafed Barges one destroyed,
Strafed Trucks, no luck hard to get at through jungle.

Ray gives us his perspective:

After the loss of Sqn Ldr Ingram the squadron moved the thirty miles to Imphal's main airfield which with the breaking of the Japanese stranglehold on the Kohima road and corresponding reduced reliance on Dakota transports had now become more available for fighter use.

It also presented less opportunity to infiltrated attack

Incidentally to give some indication of how successful the protecting squadrons had been, out of the thousands of flights carried out to sustain our troops, only twenty Dakotas were ever actually lost.

The advantages gained meant that over the past few weeks' operations have gone over more and more to the offensive, with daily bombing and strafing whenever targets presented themselves. The Japanese were very adept at camouflage and very rarely presented more than one chance to attack. Pilots, confessed Ray, said that flying over the jungle was akin to flying over the sea and after making an attack and banking round for another, invariably their target had completely disappeared as jungle swallowed everything within seconds.

These strafes were fraught with danger because of the effort required to locate the Japanese. Len writes in his log after a sweep over Shwebo on the 18th August that Warrant Officer Adcock struck a tree and was immediately killed as his Spit disappeared from view.

By the end of the month Len too had finally succumbed to the beastly bug, whether it was malaria or dysentery, or a bit of both we shall never know, for only Vicky ever let drop that Smithy left Imphal under par for treatment and convalescence. A recovery, Vicky gave us to understand some forty years later, miraculously accomplished by the intake of beer. Which itself sounded like a typical Smithy remedy. We would eventually hear of his exploits deep in the Himalayas.

By the 6th September, this time during Smithy's absence, the squadron were on the move again. Ray seems unable to recall the particular reason but whatever it was the strip still remained inside the Imphal Box, at a place called Tulihul.

The move coincided with his expected promotion to sergeant, one step which unfortunately also held the displeasing prospect of being posted away from 152. Ever since the return of Sergeant Fitter Armourer Joe O'Sullivan, Ray had always realised any advancement in his own rank would mean becoming surplus to establishment requirements. Yet somehow he could not envisage the prospect of saying goodbye to 152 after so many years and through so many campaigns.

Whatever the future held, for the moment he would keep mum with fingers crossed.

One thing he did remark upon was the elaborate state of Tulihul's domestic site, constituting as it did one of the most permanent that he'd experienced abroad. Although still of the bamboo basha type of construction, the Sergeants Mess nevertheless bordered on the luxurious.

Naturally the proverbial bar was in evidence and with Ray's Armament Officer, one Arthur Skeffington, currently acting as Mess President, it followed that as the junior sergeant, Ray would take on the duties of Squadron Barman, but it must be stated that up to this point, due more to supply than demand only soft drinks were able to be dispensed.

Life in general had improved as far as the battle for Burma was concerned, and the initiative had definitely been wrested from the Japanese, so conspiring with the officers mess, the sergeants made representation to their C/O about the possibility of acquiring beverage of the stronger variety.

One of the planes attached to each of the Spitfire squadrons was a Harvard trainer. Apart from being something used by pilots fresh from Blighty or other theatres of war to familiarise themselves with their new terrain, it also provided a useful workhorse or taxi.

The North American Harvard looked remarkably like a Japanese fighter, being similar in wing form, fuselage, and radial engine shape to the Zero or Oscar, and later during the campaign 152's particular runabout had a bizarre hair-raising escape. At this moment in time however everyone concerned managed to convince Harry to let it be used for the express purpose of acquiring real hooch from Calcutta. A request readily accepted by the Major.

It wasn't long before Ray found himself seated behind F/O Charles Dobson, without either a parachute or radio for comfort, every piece of available space being needed for the safe transportation of untold bottles of Indian Kurure gin, a product that later won outstanding approval.

The actual trip to Dum Dum airfield on the outskirts of the city and back, took them over the Ganges delta, where Ray couldn't help wondering what a miserable existence the poor natives must have endured as he looked down on mile upon mile of small rivers interspersed with mud banks and villages. Then to fly over the mountain ranges that surrounded Imphal covered as they were in a thick carpet of tropical forest. He gazed in awe contemplating the trouble types went to, to get a drink, quite certain that if they'd been forced to crash land, the resultant explosion from all the Gin they were carrying would have been akin to a blockbuster bomb.

As usual somebody managed to adopt a mascot for the mess, this time in the form of a chicken, a young cockerel as they thought whom they proceeded to call Oscar after the notorious Japanese fighter. Quite content Oscar happily roosted in the rafters, and then one day after the acquisition of the gin, Oscar suddenly laid an egg. Everyone had received a generous ration of rum on top of the gin this day, so great idiotic play was made of Oscar's egg, with their surprise finishing up taking pride of place on the bar.

As Ray remarked, 'absolutely mad but good for morale'.

About this time some of General Wingate's long range penetration boys, the Chindits, called in to see the squadron, having just returned from one of their forays, affording Ray the opportunity to learn of their exploits. He describes them as a grand, courageous, and very tough bunch.

Little or nothing was being seen of the Japanese air force from Talihul with the squadron tasked with almost an entirely offensive role.

Having failed to take India, leaving his general lines of communication stretched beyond breaking point, plus suffering from a marked lack of food and medical supplies, the Japanese at last began their long retreat. One thing they never seemed to lack though was ammunition. Quite soon now the RAF, including 152, would be ordered to follow them.

Back in Srinagar Len reminisced on his experiences to Sister Cecilia.

Hello Ciss,

Writing to you after my return from an eight day trek through to Tibet, one of the most famous passes through the Himalayas. This has been to me something I shall never forget, starting from Sonamarg we took horses and food to last us five days, killing of course a few sheep on the way.

We were walking, which in all, both there and back, is around 140 miles, covering about 20 miles a day. It really was a marvellous trek, striding along the valley where the river Sind flows, reaching a point where the Zogi-la Pass begins.

Here you see before you some eight miles distant a huge Glacier standing white against the vivid blue sky, you feel as though you are walking into a dream! A dream that everybody wishes for, as if this were the place you came to die after a hard try in the world you've left behind.

At one time I was at 10'000 feet looking into a valley 3'000 feet below surrounded by snow covered peaks. In the middle of this valley stood a small hill encircled by a stream and all around were strewn the bare bones of Yaks and Horses.

I collected one of the Skulls and wrote my name and some of my pals on it, then stuck two bones beneath to imitate the Skull and Crossbones, writing also the words, "Gone this way" this the others saw when they passed by later that day, and it was still there three days later on my return.

I would love to get into Tibet to see the Monasteries which very few ever see.

We never shaved and seldom washed as it was too damned cold, so cold in fact that I slept in my Teddy Bear jacket, including all my other clothes of course.

There was a time when we were trudging through a heavy blizzard, can you picture the scene in your minds eye! A team of six horses laden with tents, strung out behind one-another in line astern, half covered in snow.

Len continued in this vein, obviously thrilled and enchanted by these vistas and free from the constraints of censorship for the very first time.

One other bit of news would reach us from this haven of rest: his commission came through. He wrote to say that it had been over six months since his interview with his AOC (Air Officer Commanding Group). This first rate officer, Group Captain Stanley Vincent CB, DFC, AFC, DL, looking after 221 Group in SEAC of which 152 was a part, was the only RAF officer ever to have fought and won in fighter aircraft of both world wars and after thirty-five years' service, having flown no fewer than 120 types, finished up as an Air Vice Marshal.

The Air Ministry in London had apparently written back to him after some time had elapsed to enquire if he were aware that Flt Sgt Smith had struck a flagpole with his aircraft some years previously. Fortunately Vincent was able to confirm that he did, and despite this fact still recommended this NCO for commissioned rank. So at long last Smithy had finally redeemed himself, and to cap it all, so delayed had his promotion been, that within a week of his return to 152 his Pilot Officer status had transformed into Flying Officer. His greatest accolade however stemmed from the moment when even the AOC called him Smithy!

On October 20th Len was flying again, doing a thirty minute recce of their new strip at Tulihul.

One unfortunate coincidence revolved around the fact that during his absence Ray, having become a sergeant, would normally have been able to enjoy a much closer relationship with him but due to the promotional timings would remain separated at least in the social sense of the word, although Ray still fondly remembered my brother.

Before the month was out something important happened to the squadron that would remain emblazoned upon the mind of every one who ever served with 152. Just how the sequence of events evolved is, after all these years despite much research still a little hazy. But one thing of which I am assured by those with first hand knowledge, such as Ray, Norman Jones, Norman Dear, Ken Plumridge ('Plum'), Eric Clegg and certainly Major Harry Hoffe, is that Smithy was a major player.

I must apologise in advance for any error accidentally perpetrated in this telling, but I remain convinced until proven otherwise that Sergeant Pilot Geoff Duval of 152 saw a painting of a small black panther on the nose cone of a Dakota – wherever, it was certainly something that gelled in his mind, and to which he referred in direct discussion with Smithy, and possibly Bluey Herman.

At the time, Ray recalls, there had been much talk in the squadron of the lack of publicity afforded 152 by various media such as the *SEAC News* or *The Times of India*. It aggrieved them a little to say the least when reports centred almost exclusively around squadrons in the 600 range. Any ideas, everyone agreed, would be worth considering if it brought 152 more to the fore.

Before long Len together with Bluey and Geoff approached Harry. Aware of my brother's artistry coupled with the jogging of distant memories, it would not be unfair to suggest that Smithy produced a painting of a MkVIII Spit showing a large Black Panther complete with white edging and mean-looking eye, spread-eagled over the fuselage port roundel in a leaping posture.

The effect looked decidedly striking, and when studying Spitfire squadron markings from the Second World War, nowhere have I seen such an imposing study.

During his reminiscences Eric Clegg, then one of the NCOs supping at the The Odd Nogg Inne, Ray's 'Mess Bar', said, and I quote, 'How could I ever have forgotten Donald Duck, and I wonder whatever happened to the life size pin up bathing beauty he painted on fabric to brighten up the Sergeants Mess!'

Immediately Harry was impressed, giving his outright blessing for the Cat to be installed, after all without being dishonourable you couldn't do a great deal with the Nizam's Hat, their current emblem.

No time was lost, with all three proudly producing a six foot long stencil, capable of being transferred to the fuselage, and before you could say 'tally ho' the Black Panthers of Burma were born.

Ray put it admirably when he remarked, 'It caught everyone's eye, including the propaganda people.'

After the war I do know that Len took it upon himself to replace their lapel badge with one showing the black cat as opposed to the hat, and that without this new squadron marking that so easily concentrates the mind many a meeting would not have happened and this history would have been short of material in important aspects.

Managing another six hours of Rhubarbs during this last week of October Len quickly settled into the swing of things, until on the 29th everyone flew to Tamu, just across the border, to claim the distinction of being the first squadron to re-enter Burma.

Tamu lay in the Kabaw Valley, with the road from Imphal to Tamu, (if it could be called that!) pushed through the jungle over a considerable range of hills, mountains in some cases, by the engineers, and although it wasn't far as the crow flies it took several hours on the ground. From this point it became even more difficult to move by truck until well south of Mandalay, as there was practically no metalled roads and from November 1944 until January '45 the monsoon rains added to their problems. After that, said Ray, it would be dust that invaded everywhere as at that time they were in the dry hot centre of Burma, that is until June, when it would turn to mud again.

For the next six months or so the airstrips they occupied would start out as small affairs carved from virgin jungle to accommodate light aircraft like Stinson L-5s, utilised for evacuating wounded, and only later enlarged for the use of fighter squadrons.

One of their prime duties from Tamu included the defence of the bridgehead over the Chindwin, and the Bailey bridge at Kelwa. This latter was the longest in the world at that time and continual patrols were the order of the day and would be for some time. The Japanese did attempt to attack but received a bloody nose, and no hits were recorded. The river here ran very deep and fast due to heavy rainfall in the mountains, and this alone produced the imperative that nothing nasty should befall the bridge.

Maps used by pilots marked the country for many miles around, in fact hundreds of square miles, as 'Reserve Forest', and when able to walk through you realised why, for it consisted of massive if not absolutely giant teak trees, which in pounds sterling must have been valued in millions.

Ray couldn't help relating the jungle atmosphere when opposed to Hollywood movies, where scenes depicted screeching of birds and constant animal noises. In truth, he said, you could walk for miles through this type of jungle and never hear so much as a whisper. The silence at times was absolute. Only around and about the water holes would you be able to find evidence or actually see wildlife. He did recall seeing a colony of monkeys once when moving camp, they had collected near a small stream, but this was the only time he ever witnessed such phenomena.

Since the bail-out and repatriation of Flt Lt Norman Jones, A Flight seems to have been led first by F/O 'Dook' Allington, then by Smithy himself and finally by Flt Lt Francis, although another Flt Lt Jones does show in Len's log and this particular entry is shown on Guy Fawkes Day. The caption recorded is a scramble at first light on 5th November 1944, and reads: 'Mixed it with 12 plus Zero's, Destroyed one, Damaged one. Flt Lt Jones got a probable,- whizo scrap !'

Fortunately Vicky was able some forty years later to fill me in on a few of the details:

Both flights were scrambled, and we in B Flight had seen piss all, so there we were 12,000 feet above, watching Smithy race back to base, having run out of ammo, falling out of C for Charlie's cockpit and proceeding to perform idiotic handstands, while two of the Nips who had followed now shot up the old homestead.

Len wrote home to our Sister Ciss two days later on the seventh November the following is an extract from that letter:

Well I'm back with the Sqdn again just like being home again. It's a wizard Sqdn we've moved since I last went on leave sorry can't tell you where. Been having bags of fun since my return luck being all the way with me perhaps I could put it like this, you know that song about Johnny got a "O" well you can put Len there now in its place I also damaged one not bad eh. I'll soon get that baker's dozen that Jack asked for.

Yet another threshold had been crossed, as Len became one of only six RAF pilots to account for aircraft belonging to all three Axis powers: German, Italian, and Japanese. This fact was elaborated upon by Ray as he entered his ninety-first year in 2011 – he challenges anyone to dispute that Brother Len was the only Englishman to do so whilst serving within the same squadron!

Occasionally Ray and a couple of his mates scouted afield with shotguns in search of game to supplement RAF rations. Very often they found that late in the day pigeons and jungle fowl tended to congregate around the open spaces created by the Burmese as cultivation areas. Each time they ventured in threes, the idea being to lie quietly in wait on the jungle's edge until sensing safety the birds settled to feed, then their guns fired in unison.

He remembers vividly that one kind of pigeon sported yellow feathers, bit like a canary, a particularly plump variety. Jungle fowl were the most prized, definitely the forerunner of our domestic chicken, weighing in at five or six pounds, very tasty and well worth the shot, could be a rather elusive target though.

On one occasion having settled down to this exercise with everything eerily quiet, there was suddenly one hell of a commotion exceedingly close by, coupled with screaming and trumpeting, a furore that turned out to be an elephant tethered by natives on the jungle's edge. 'We high tailed it to our bashas for a change of underwear,' chuckles Ray.

A week before Xmas members of the squadron were trying hard to ascertain if anything special was likely to be laid on in the way of nosh, and when little or nothing seemed to be in the offing Ray made the tentative suggestion that perhaps a few of them may be permitted to journey to the lake at Imphal for the express purpose of winning some game for the mess table.

Extracting permission from good old Harry, Ray's armoury officer W/O Skevington, together with Flt Sgt 'Lofty' Halls from Signals, and Ray himself commandeered a small truck and set off on the full day's journey for a wildfowl shoot on Lake Logtac.

The size of the shot to be used was of paramount importance, as the guns used by squadron pilots to keep their eye in when not flying only contained cartridges with number six or eight shot. If they were to bag any geese, which they were hoping for, lead shot of at least number four size would be needed, this they discovered was exactly the size of lead used in the process of parachute packing (bags of shot were used to weigh down the lines and canopy while folding them), so before making tracks some hours were spent removing one size of shot for the bigger variety.

This safari would last three days, one to get there, one for the shoot and one for the return journey. On arrival three dug out canoes were quickly organised including of course three local types to operate them.

Being considerably chilly of a morning they'd each taken the precaution of packing a bivouac, and to sustain themselves squeezed in some bully and bread too. Washing and shaving had to be performed in the icy lake water.

Dug-out canoes are notoriously unstable which Ray quickly discovered when fortunately in shallow water he took his first poop side ways on. The sudden recoil upended everyone and everything, leaving both he and his helper looking damn silly bang on their butts and soaking wet. From this point on firing would only take place when the canoe itself actually pointed its nose at the target.

To get to deeper water and the game they were after, each guide had to navigate through thick, high dense rushes, which grew all round the perimeter. Prior to this exercise it was impossible to see the actual lake, so it struck them with some surprise when they did break through to see the tremendous expanse and extent of its blackness, implying rather a considerable depth, and them without lifejackets in a wobbly hollowed-out tree. Ray noted they hadn't thought to bring their Mae Wests and found the venture a little daunting.

However, each guide showed adroitness at placing their canoes exactly where required to overcome any tendency to capsize. The other surprise as margin rushes were breached was the numbers of water fowl, not hundreds, but literally thousands of birds, Grey Lag, Pink Feet, Bar Head Geese, duck and teal. They learnt later that the whole area acted as a winter stopover from lakes in southern Russia each bird having to fly over the Himalayan range. The lake surface was littered with floating islands of vegetation, with these being liberally populated by the wildfowl.

No sooner had they spotted their pursuers than many of the birds would take off for the far side of the lake, especially after hearing the first fusillade, which encouraged frantic paddling from the oarsman. Ray found the honking and wing noise exceptionally impressive.

At the day's end their truck was filled, but it was not something Ray would ever do again. These birds had never seen a gun before, and the results achieved were not something he would boast about. His one excuse, he said, was to supply the squadron with something special for Xmas dinner, as it turned out the powers that be had organised festive food so everyone was forced to consume their bag beforehand.

After Christmas Len wrote that things had gone okay on his side of the world.

On the day of course everybody got stinko, even before we had dinner.
I being the longest serving pilot attached to our Squadron had to
make a speech but couldn't really collate my thoughts, for the speech

before had been given by a pilot that used to be my number two before in time he became a number one.

He toasted me together with the rest of the boys, saying things that made me feel so proud to be amongst the greatest types one could wish for.

He talked about having the greatest admiration for a pilot that not one person on the Squadron wouldn't follow.

That's wonderful to know that, I know I could go anywhere and still have the boys behind me, no matter what the task.

Its New Year now, and with any luck I hope to see the next one in Blighty.

Travelling from Imphal a Flying Officer known to most as 'Plum' (real name Kenneth Plumridge) journeyed valiantly to reach Tamu by Christmas, but the abominable weather and terrain caused him to miss 152's celebrations, much to his chagrin! Having recently transferred from the Middle East, Plum actually flew from the Waterloo strip next door to Paddington during the Tunisian campaign, before later becoming seconded to training command, giving valuable instruction on the trusty North American Harvard.

Fifty-three years later we met because of the Black Panthers, whereupon among other things it was discovered he and his squadron had acted as top cover the day Smithy was involved in the bombing of Comiso's salt factory. Also through Plum I met Ray and from then on others who served with 152. This meeting requires a few paragraphs of its own, if only to accentuate the value of that endearing cat.

My youngest sister Irene desired a painting of our brother's favourite Spitfire, namely C for Charlie (referred to above by Vicky, observing Len cavorting round on his hands celebrating his latest victory). She commissioned the painting from an amateur artist who happened to be a work friend of her husband. Many years later, in 1997 to be precise, the artist decided to hold an exhibition in his local town hall at Hornchurch in Essex. To complement other works he reproduced a second painting of C for Charlie viewed from the port side, complete with Panther. One day a distinguished-looking inquisitive type enquired after the artist. Having received the requisite information, immediately he proceeded to make contact.

'Of all the Spitfires,' he quizzed, 'why did you paint that one?'

'Because,' said the artist, 'I rather liked it, having been commissioned by the pilot's sister for the original.'

'Do you know anything about her brother?' asked the gentleman.

'I believe he was involved in some sort of accident in Scotland,' came the reply.

Immediately his enquirer let out a gasp. 'My god!' he exclaimed, 'that's Smithy's plane!'

Of course the distinguished gentleman with tousled grey hair and moustache was none other than Ken Plumridge, who wasted little time in contacting my sister, and the rest swiftly became another twist to history.

After Christmas, Ray tells us, the weather turned particularly bad, with monsoon-type storms coming in from the Bay of Bengal, and because of these rains Twelfth Night came easily to mind.

Through Tamu and the rest of their travels within Burma they all lived entirely in tents with the Sergeants Mess quartered inside its own marquee. To increase their defence against possible air attack, ground levels were dug down about two feet six inches before erecting the canvas, and extra slit trenches carved. As you can imagine after about a week of monsoon weather everyone was busting their insides trying to keep what sparse accommodation they had dry.

There they were in the Mess marquee feeling absolutely miserable, wearing wellies or flying boots, draped in waterproof capes, anything to keep the confounded water out while they imbibed a few bevies. Suddenly someone yelled out that it was twelfth night, so damp bodies started to sing and dance, gradually getting more boisterous, moving tables and chairs, kicking off boots, removing wellies and socks throwing aside capes, anything that might be difficult to clean as the mud was churned up in one hilarious uproar. What a night, what a pissy, what a mad, mad, lot, what a time to remember! – The beginning of 1945 on the edge of Burma!

Before long, while spirits were high, letters would be sent to Bing Crosby, Bob Hope and Dorothy Lamour. Ray never remembered what form the letters to Crosby and Hope took, but he did remember they asked Dorothy Lamour for one of her spare sarongs! They never got one of course, but they did get a reply along with a signed photograph. A souvenir that took pride of place in the Mess for many a long day.

War went on and by the 15th January Harry was winging his pilots 110 miles straight south to a place called Kan. A position slightly north of, but about 120 miles west of Mandalay.

Quite soon after their arrival another pilot would be lost over the treacherous terrain whilst flying through the constant heavy cumulus. This time a fellow countryman of Harry's, Lieutenant L G Potgieter, from South Africa, who had been part of B Flight when Harry commanded it way back in Baigachi days. Vicky as their flight reporter would break the news to Len. Harry was reaching repatriation, and it must have been highly likely that the lost South African had also stood in similar stead.

But before Major Hoffe relinquished his command he was able to perform one final pleasant duty, requesting Len see him in order to convey news of his, Smithy's, decoration. No previous member of 152 had ever been awarded the DFM, plenty of DFCs to officers, but not the other. Given whilst still an NCO it needed to be won more quickly. Coupled with it came two congratulatory telegrams: one dated 22nd January 1945 arrived from S F Vincent CB, DFC, AFC, DL, their AOC commanding 221 Group, and one dated 19th January came from Air Marshal Sir Guy Garrod, KCB, OBE, MC, DFC, Allied Air Commander-in-Chief, South East Asia.

As Major Hoffe DFC prepared to sail home for a well deserved rest, so Sqn Ldr Grant 'Gary' Kerr DFC took command of 152, which although not realised at the time would be the final commander to carry the squadron through to war's end and outright victory.

Gary had won his decoration leading a flight of twin-engine Beaufighters over the English Channel, in an attack on those elusive battleships *Scharnhorst* and *Gneisenau* as they made a final desperate dash from Brest harbour. These fast, highly manoeuvrable, powerful battleships had been kept holed up in Brest for ten months until their breakout on the 12th February 1942. Altogether over 4,000 tons of bombs had been dropped for the loss of forty-three aircraft and 247 crew, not forgetting 152's well loved Ace, Eric 'Boy' Marrs, of course.

During their dash through the Channel some 600 aircraft pursued them for five hours, including torpedo-carrying Swordfish and Beaufighters, of which Gary's plane was one. British warships also took part to harry the Germans during the hours of darkness. At the end both enemy battleships were seen to limp towards Heligoland Bight. Despite bad visibility pilots were confident both major vessels had been struck, with the enemy admitting to the loss of one patrol vessel and one large torpedo boat. Six Swordfish were lost, plus a further twenty bombers and sixteen fighters, against German aircraft losses of eighteen. Somehow these powerful boats had to be deterred from entering

Allied shipping lanes.

As January drew to a close, Ray was glad that at last Burmese weather started to improve. From now on though and for several months to come as they entered this dry season, they would be forced to wear long slacks, boots and gaiters, as a precaution against scrub typhus. Certainly the order declaring compulsory intake of mepacrine had virtually eliminated the dreaded malaria.

About this time Lord Louis Mountbatten paid the squadron a visit; as chief of SEAC the supremo liked to pay calls to his various commands, bringing everyone whenever prudent up to date with the latest state of affairs, and just where exactly he was hoping they would all be going and how soon.

Len had been carrying out many escort duties of late and no doubt some of these related to His Lordship. Certainly he wrote of meeting a big cheese, which one day on his return home he would tell us about. There is no doubt subsequently that Lord Mountbatten knew and met Len personally whilst in Burma. Ray refers to his pep-talk and congratulations on everybody doing a good job.

He spoke intensely on how his original intention had been to invade Rangoon from the sea and so catch the Japs in a pincer movement, but said they would now drive down from the north to take Burma, pushing on without stopping not even for the monsoons. A declaration, says Ray that held true after fighting through one monsoon, through a dry season and into another monsoon before the Japanese finally capitulated.

Enemy aircraft appeared to be virtually non-existent at this time and 152's duties became almost exclusively close support to Allied ground troops. They would attack targets nominated by them, and later became so organised in this field that they instituted a system called cab rank, whereby Spitfires and Hurribombers would queue up to attack targets directed by an RAF officer on the ground, who sometimes signalled his instructions from within only yards of the enemy positions.

Occasionally the odd Japanese aircraft got through to carry out a sneak attack, one such being before they left Tamu, when shortly after an American Mitchell bomber had landed it disappeared in a pile of wreckage alongside a similarly fated Spitfire.

The weather now showed signs of becoming very hot and dry, and soon the Gangaw valley where Kan was situated became a dust bowl. 'So dusty,' complained Ray, 'that immediately after the first Spitty had taken off in the

morning, everyone and everything was coated in dust for the rest of the day.'
Making maintenance, as he so poignantly emphasised 'b---dy difficult'.

Just to cheer them up, at long last a concert party arrived. In the European
Theatre these were fairly frequent, but out here in the heat and jungle it took
very dedicated types to venture into forward areas to entertain our boys.
They were not famous or well known, said Ray, but their enthusiasm and
friendliness was very much appreciated by one and all.

Within a short space of time it became Sqn Ldr Gary Kerr's turn to wend
152 to a new destination, this time reaching a strip further south and nearer
the Irrawaddy River called Sinthe by 7th February. Here IV Corps, of the
Fourteenth Army, would effect a crossing close to the ancient capital of
Pagan (now called Bagan), a Burmese city full of pagodas.

Patrols and strafes continued unabated, with pilots sometimes airborne
three times in a day to harry the enemy as IV Corps pushed relentlessly south.

In between these sorties Len also took turn at being grog runner, to collect
152's gin supply from Calcutta, invariably managing to wangle Vicky as his
helper. The two of them had struck up a relationship with a chap called Ian
Stephens, none other than the Chief Editor of India's renowned newspaper,
the *New Statesman*, and at this gentlemen's invitation invariably stayed at his
Calcutta flat. Unfortunately I have not been able to trace any cuttings, but I
feel sure that Vicky and Len would have been instrumental in procuring news
coverage for 152 through this friendship. Certainly Ian thought highly of Len
as expressed in later correspondence from Stephens to our sister Cecilia.

It was on the evening of the thirteenth that Len decided to write home,
reaching a point of explanation to Ciss of how hot and humid their current
climate was, so much so he was emphasising, it made it hard for one to think
– and suddenly something caused him to stop in mid-sentence.

The reason, it transpired, was one helluva commotion (as Ray tells it)
of a Japanese sneak raider dropping a stick of fragmentation bombs. Over
the weeks, Ray felt, they had possibly become lulled into a false sense of
security with little or no activity directed towards them, so this episode was
all the more devastating. The lone bomber had apparently latched onto some
of our own homeward-bound bomber aircraft without detection and was thus
guided right onto the unsuspecting target.

Night had just fallen at about 8.00 pm with crews settling back into their
tented billets.

One bomb, says Ray, struck their corporals' tent; he felt unable to recall

all those that were lost, but certainly Corporals Bill Taggert, Wally Swift and Jock McRobert were killed, along with Jock Halliday. How many more, including their names, have been lost to memory, I don't know, but many more there certainly were. It was a disastrous and heartrending time for all, and of course there were large numbers injured who needed to be cared for.

Ray's memoirs include photographs of the wounded in hospital, as well as a small patch of hallowed ground close by Sinthe Air Strip where the boys were laid to rest. He couldn't help but note the unfortunate date of the 13th, with the burial next day taking place on Valentines Day.

This day, the 14th February 1945, also became noted for another event, and if I may I should like to add a little anecdote.

During the mid-1980s I wrote my brother's biography, called *Smithy*, and appreciating his artistry, along with his NCO seniority status when reaching Biagachi, India, I fictionally had him quizzing other NCO pilots on Japanese aircraft recognition. Knowing the similarity of the North American Harvard, used as squadron runabouts, to the Jap fighters, I portrayed him showing others his drawing of the tail end of a Harvard and inviting them to distinguish the aircraft. On each occasion his compatriots would diagnose a particular enemy fighter, upon which Len would proclaim mischievously, 'Remind me not to fly the squadron Harvard when you buggers are aloft!!'

And indeed, on the 14th February 152's Harvard was shot down by a Spitfire from 17 Squadron. Wherein lies the adage, 'Truth is stranger than fiction'.

At the time Ray knew very little about the pilot or his passenger, or the attacker, except that the passenger was an official photographer bound for the Irrawaddy to obtain pictures of the bridgehead being forged across the river under a heavy smokescreen, and that the Harvard crash-landed. Both occupants survived.

After meeting Ray at Duxford in 1998 he sent me photocopies of a letter from Flt Lt Donald K Healey who flew with 17 Squadron, under the effective command of the well known and flamboyant J H 'Ginger' Lacey DFM & bar, Croix de Guerre. (These copies Ray himself had received in December 1992 and were included with material received from both F/O Harry Ashley, the official photographer, who incidentally ended up as Chief Photographer to my local paper the *Bournemouth Echo*) and Flt Lt Ken Rutherford DFC of 17 Squadron who wrote from New Zealand about his friend Rathwell the unfortunate Spitfire pilot associated with the incident. (Flt Lt Donald K

Healey I also discovered lived close by at Poole, a gentleman I managed to converse over the phone with, despite his recent heart attack.)

Harry writes:

Time dims the memory, and it is only with the aid of Logbooks that the true facts of those unforgettable days in the jungle can safely be recalled.

As a RAF Official Photographer I had to link up with Air Force units to produce pictures for the World press, and my two years in the Far East, which covered the re-taking of Mandalay, Rangoon and Singapore were packed with excitement.

I recall covering the Hump crossing into Kun-Ming with Sqn Ldr Wort in a Dakota, and a more dramatic journey over these mountains with an American Capt Stratford who was flying a Dak solo for CNAC with a u/s radio. I was over Rangoon on day one and two in a Mosquito piloted by F/Lt Brown an ex Chindit. We dropped the last bomb on Rangoon.

The name of Capt Saito still sends a chill down my back because this English University educated Jap, an ex airline pilot, announced to me that he had recently volunteered as a suicide pilot as we took off in a Topay on a Potatoe run from Saigon, after hostilities had ceased.

It was an odd coincidence that after the war Don Healy was searching the World for pictures of 'Jimmie Nuttie', when I, who took them was living within two miles of Don.

Of that traumatic day, the 14th Feb. 1945 my log book reads.

06.30 Took off in Harvard piloted by F/O Jackson '152 Sqdn' to photograph smoke screen laid over the Irrawaddy to cover 14th Army crossing. Mistaken for an Oscar by a covering Spitfire of 17 Sqdn piloted by F/O Rathwell and shot down. Pilot wounded in head and myself in arm, side and foot. Made a successful crash landing. Duration 1 hour.

Before I arrived in Burma I had been flying in daylight raids in Lancasters over Caen and LeHavre with 166 Sqdn and the ritual of take-off on an English bomber station was in sharp contrast to the systems used on jungle airstrips.

The decision to make this trip was made at the last minute, and when the Aldis lamp winked us an OK I doubt weather any other Sqdn had been notified of our take-off, and the nature of our mission.

I remember the Spitfire coming astern of us and suddenly Jacko slumped over the controls and I saw blood oozing through his helmet. Although there was a hole right through my arm, I felt no pain and had no idea that I had been hit until after we had landed and I found my sleeve soaked in blood. The force of air in descent brought the pilot to consciousness and pulling back the stick he glided us down and our landing was cushioned by some tall grasses.

We disembarked very quickly and discovered that a shell fragment had cut open Jacko's helmet, cut the skin and stunned him.

As we walked away he said, 'we ought to have a picture'. So we returned for me to photograph him kneeling on the wing.

We were evacuated from a MDS by L5 'Sgt Fudge' and later returned from Sinthe to Onbauk in another Harvard.

If memory serves me correctly The Group Captain ordered 17 Sqdn to send their Harvard to 152 Sqdn.

We hoped that Rothwell would fly over to apologise and we could have had a party,----- but we never met.

Although I have dined on the story over the years my newspaper colleagues never believed the line shoot and the recent disclosure of the incident in your Sqdn Magazine '17 Sqdn' gave proof at last.

The Evening Echo Bournemouth printed the story under the headline 'Its official--- He really was shot down'.

Flt Lt Ken Rutherford wrote to Don Healy in November 1983:

Dear Don
Thanks for all the guff and stuff which as always was most interesting and I'm writing promptly in reply as I was very close to the shooting down of the 152 Squadron Harvard in the Burma Campaign.

It was on the 14th February 1945 very early in the morning that I took two sections of two Spitfires each of 17 Sqdn down to the Pakokku area to cover the crossing of the Irrawaddy river by the 7th Division, which actually took place during the night 13th/14th February and we arrived just as dawn was breaking.

This was a very hush hush operation as it was essential that the Japs had no warning and even I as a Flight Commander knew nothing about it until I saw it happening in spite of being one of the close support Squadrons.

As you recall, our C/O Ginger Lacey could be very secretive at times and we had only been warned by Group Ops to look out for low flying enemy aircraft in the area. So Canadian F/O Rathwell leading Blue section with Flt Sgt Gibby Gibson as his No 2 was to patrol at 2,000 feet whilst my Green section was at 20,000 feet to prevent any interference from Japs higher up.

Rath and I had been having a bit of a wager on who was going to shoot down the first enemy aircraft and that was in my mind as suddenly over the R/T came an excited Rathwell 'I've got one, Green one—pause—Bollocks it's a Harvard.'

It was a very dejected Rathwell that returned to our strip at Iwadon Nr Monywa.

Both he and his Canadian friend Bill Fell came from somewhere near Winnipeg and were attached to 17 Sqdn while they were awaiting repatriation and had previously been together on 81 Sqdn which came from the Middle East and was actively supporting Wingates sorties behind the Jap lines.

They were both excellent pilots to have around and Raths DFC came through just at this time but unfortunately the thrill of that was dulled by the mistake and his grounding which followed and I don't think he flew with us again.

I only hope that his good name was kept clean as to my mind he was in no way to blame.

As far as I know, the 152 Harvard shot down did not have the broad white strips across the wings that all allied aircraft was supposed to have. It would have been the only radial engine aircraft in the forward area and did not have IFF 'Indication Friend or Foe', or it was not switched on and that made it a 'hostile'

We had been given no information that it would be in the area, and to tag on behind a couple of Hurricanes who were low level bombing was asking for trouble. Add to this the considerable amount of smoke laid down in the early dawn to cover the crossing and the Harvard crew were very lucky to have survived at all.

As you and Don Leighton were operational with us at the time *you must remember the stink that followed and how we all stuck up for Rathwell in the enquiry.*

I have a feeling that our C/O would have seen the episode as a secret victory over 152 Spitfire Squadron with whom we had close rivalry, as we could still fly our Harvard to stock up with Gin from Calcutta and they couldn't.

Group told him to give our Harvard to 152, but we compromised and shared the Gin instead!

To Harry Ashley the photographer in the Harvard I have not yet met, I offer my sympathies on the episode, but if I had been at the low level end I would have done the same, anyhow he has a wonderful dining out story, or maybe drinking out story, so he can be happy in the thought that he is still around after being shot down by a Spitfire and living to tell the tale.

As an epilogue to this story, I remember seeing written somewhere that after investigation it was determined that only sixteen bullets were missing from Rathwell's magazines.

On this day, 14th February Len's log book shows two patrols over the Sinthe area, one flying Spitfire K for King and the second in C for Charlie, his favourite, and it was whilst on this patrol he reported F/O Jones destroyed one Dinah. Three days later whilst patrolling the same area B Flight were lucky enough to bump into a group of Oscars and dove into them with devastating results, with once again Len recording the outcome.

F/O John Willoughby Vickers destroyed one Oscar, Flt Sgt Unsead destroyed one Oscar, and Flt Lt Francis along with F/O Gus damaging two each and F/O Jones damaging another.

Altogether two down and five damaged without loss to ourselves.

A fitting outcome after the dreadful loss's sustained on the thirteenth.

Without a doubt February 1945 was turning into a busy and eventful month, so much so that on the 25th 152's C/O Gary Kerr received a telegram from Louis Mountbatten.

My dear Kerr

I am very grateful to you and your Squadron for providing fighter cover for me when I was down in your area recently, and I shall be most grateful if you would pass on a special word of thanks to Flying Officer Smith and other pilots who flew with him.

I am afraid that our rendezvous in the early hours of the morning did not come off, but that was entirely because we were several minutes ahead of schedule

You and the other Squadrons in your area certainly seem to be on top of the Jap these days, as whenever I hear that enemy aircraft have been up over our lines you seem to dispose of about half their number.

Good luck to you

Yours sincerely

Louis Mountbatten

[From the author: See memoir of W/O Ernie Unstead within the photo section.]

At about this time, the very thing that Ray had been dreading came to the surface. A posting to some 'Jungle Target Research Establishment' of all things. To seasoned Ray it sounded like a horrible backwoods sort of unit, as hastily he conjured a way to get around the directive. Arranging a meeting with the C/O as soon as practicable.

Convincingly he pleaded with Gary to let him stay with 152 the only unit he had known and come to love since his inception into squadron service. He even argued that with the way things were going the wars end could be in sight. 'Why!' he contended, 'the whole campaign could be over before I even get to wherever this new place is.'

Gary needed little encouragement to agree with his Sergeant Armourer certainly at this late stage it would be foolish to lose the expertise of such a valued member of the squadron. Ray stayed put, and when later one of the armament officers came round from Wing or possibly Group carrying out the usual checks, he was at pains to know why 152 were still over their complement of sergeants in the Armoury section and hadn't 'he' (meaning Ray) received posting orders.

Quickly Ray resorted to subterfuge, explaining with tongue firmly in cheek, that no such order had been received, and once again emphasised the point that hostilities may soon be over and there seemed little value in moving around now. In any event after this meeting nothing further happened and Ray gave a sigh of relief when everyone finally left him alone to see out the war with 152.

Throughout March the squadron would be patrolling and strafing, protecting the bridgehead with Len mostly at the controls of C for Charlie, and their next move when it came in April would be without him. A patrol over Pagan on 30th March became his final front line duty and association with 152.

Having arrived at Souk-el-Khemis on 16th March 1943 he had now completed more than two years' service with one squadron. Arriving as a sergeant with a serious Black against his character he would be leaving as a well loved member with the rank of Flying Officer and holder of 152's only DFM.

His record included:

Five and a half aircraft destroyed in the air, with one probable and two damaged.

Two further aircraft destroyed on the ground.

One oil tanker damaged.

Four motor-launches and two barges destroyed.

Twenty-eight trucks destroyed.

Eighteen sampans destroyed.

Everyone would give him a well-deserved send-off, with Gary writing a nice summary inside his logbook, thanking him for everything he had done for the squadron.

So well was the send off with more bevies being imbibed in Calcutta that Len failed to appreciate that as senior officer on the train he actually commanded it. Able to issue orders to stop and start the beast as he wished. His first problem encountered took the form of an Alexander nurse who was Irish and stubborn with it, insisting on holding up the train every time they stopped for a meal at the station. After some rearrangement with the carriages Len found himself ensconced with this maverick, and it didn't help matters when she discovered some clever clogs had chalked outside their compartment 'O.C. Train & Wife'.

His destination was the very elite air station at Peshawar and the journey would take four days. The rest of this story is left to everyone's imagination. But in fairness to Len he did leak the episode eventually to sister Ciss, emphasising strongly that nothing improper took place.

I give you part of his letter written from 151 OTU Peshawar, SEAAF (South East Asia Air Force):

Well Ciss over this side of the world it's still too hot but apart from that everything's O.K. I get more flying hrs in just lately. Hey! I must tell you this you'll think I'm a bad lad but it's all in the fun of life. When I left Calcutta saying goodbye to the gang I was a bit worse for the weather on entering the train. Next morning I found sheets of paper with bags of bumff on either side. It suddenly dawned on me I was c/o of the train mind you the whole of the train I could stop and start it when I pleased. This was good so I thought, but for a nurse who always seemed to be the last for meals, I having to hold the train up at each stop. The only thing I could do then was to take her to meals myself to keep an eye on her if you get what I mean. But then another big snag came along I had to change coaches also her-only one compartment was left and she had to get in with me. I find afterwards she hadn't got a ticket and when I thought of mine I found also I hadn't got one either. My! What a mess and I'm c/o of the train too. One station before the last one the ticket chappy came on and the girl took to her heels and locked herself in the lavatory, so you can imagine how much talking I had to do. The ticket chappy mentioned Memsaab which means my wife. At first I didn't catch on until he'd left the train and a Lt asked me about letting my wife out. I didn't quite get this until he told me to take a look see outside the coach, which I did and found chalked up "O.C. train and wife". What a mess here I am no ticket neither her I am o/c train and she is my wife.

Its ok you can breathe I got out of that one pretty quick. So now I often write to my wife who's up in the hills at present. She's Irish so you can guess how mad she is. No I'm not falling for her just pals.

This journey by the way took four days I don't want to hear you say. Oh yes oh yes oh yes. I was on the level no kid.

Well here's to next time xxx Len xx

He would remain at Peshawar giving air tests to the F Mk VIII until sent once more across the breadth of India, to Armada Road and the AFTU to take a Fighter Leaders course preparatory to becoming a Flight Lieutenant.

Back at 152 however much still needed to be accomplished and Ray tells of their next move, which took them across the Irrawaddy at Pakaku. 'The river at this point,' he explains, 'is about 2,000 yards wide, that's well over a mile, and believe me on a Bailey bridge that long you feel very vulnerable, especially when traversing the middle section.'

They found their way to Magwe, codenamed 'Maidavale', adjacent to the Yennanyaung oil fields, and it didn't appear that the Japanese had extracted any oil whatsoever from the wells during their occupation of Burma.

'By now,' Ray says, 'the enemy was in full retreat and suffering from poor physical condition, with lack of food and poor medical supplies being the main problems. But he never seemed to be short of ammunition, and on occasion would apparently stop and fight to the last.'

Although not actually directly related to 152, I'm sure Don Healy wouldn't mind me quoting some of his words to give a better indication of life at this time in the jungles of Burma. The sequence relates to the push south towards Mandalay. A part of the Burma operation which Smithy just missed. Speaking of 17 Squadron, Don relates how they started to fly down from Ywadon to operate during the day from a forward strip 100 miles away at Meiktila, which itself was the scene of some very fierce battles. Over 5,000 Japanese troops were killed during the struggle for control of this strategic area.

Two sections of aircraft would head for Meiktila before dawn, and whilst a pair would journey out on patrol over the bomb-line once over the battle zone, the remaining Spitfires would be employed strafing Japanese positions immediately around the strip in order to help the RAF Regiment on the ground secure the airfield.

Every night for about three weeks, Japanese commandos would take control of Meiktila's dirt runway until beaten back into the jungle at dawn by Allied troops breaking out of their 'defensive box'.

Once the strip had been recaptured, the dead Japanese that lay strewn across the site were cleared off, and the pilots quickly given the signal to land.

Once on the ground the aircraft would re-arm and refuel, and then wait for the section on patrol to return.

After two hours the Spitfires would duly appear overhead, and the pair on the ground would take off and head out on patrol leaving the recently arrived fighters to take their place at Meiktila to refuel and re-arm.

This pattern of operations would continue until dusk, when the Spitty's would return to Ywadon and our troops re-enter the security of their defensive box, when once more the Jap commandos would re-take the strip.

During the battle for Meiktila the Japanese troops would collect the scalps of dead Gurkhas for trophies, so the Gurkhas retaliated by lopping off the heads of the Japanese and mixing them up so their ancestors wouldn't recognise them in heaven, and to save their own trip to Allah the Gurkhas shaved their heads leaving a small tuft by which they themselves could be lifted to their final resting place.

It was then that Ginger Lacey and the rest of 17 Squadron did the same in honour of these brave fighting men who were guarding them at Meiktila.

Ray continues: 'Each day the 14th Army would issue bulletins on the previous days fighting. Casualties would be something like: 874 enemy killed, nine prisoners taken, or 1124 killed, seventeen prisoners taken, 260 killed, five prisoners taken. As a matter of fact the most prisoners taken at any one time was fifty-seven and more than 100,000 were killed altogether.'

The low figure of prisoners taken, Ray reckoned, could have been of their own making, although he had to agree that it was difficult enough for the Allies trying to feed their own forces. The Japs, he says, were given no respite and Allied aircraft would be told to strike a village where they were holed up, and they would be too shattered to flee.

Magwe and the Anvenyon are in the Central Burmese Desert, and at this time of the year nearing the height of the summer the temperature could soar to over 100 degrees Fahrenheit in the shade, that's if you could find any. On one occasion Ray returned to his tent which had the bottom rolled up for air circulation, only to find a very venomous Snake indeed, he could tell immediately as he approached that it was a Russell's Viper. Beating a hasty retreat he returned some time later to find to his relief that the deadly creature had disappeared. Of all the snakes he'd encountered in the Far East this had been the most dangerous.

Whilst referring to snakes Ray makes note that from their position on the desert plain they could see across the dry scrub to a 5,000 feet extinct volcano known as Mount Popa. This it was reputed was home to the King Cobra. Whether true or just myth Ray was unsure, but speaking with one ex-152 pilot since the war he seemed to substantiate the story, so it could be true.

They moved yet again to a strip at Thedaw, just south of Mandalay, where news came through that the war in Europe had finally ended. Of course they were all greatly relieved to hear this, knowing loved ones back home would now be safe. But for themselves somehow everyone started to act more cautiously. Now all they had to do was stay in one piece until they too could join in the peaceful celebrations back home.

It needed to be appreciated that front lines in Burma were really non-existent. So difficult was the terrain and rapid the advance, consisting as it did of a number of thrusts, that quite frequently the enemy could be on your flanks or even behind you. These pockets could take some time to liquidate and many of the close support units such as 152 could be in dangerous areas.

Soon after the cessation of hostilities in Europe opportunities arose for a spot of leave. Lots had to be drawn to determine the lucky ones and Ray managed to find himself amongst a party of five or six flying out of Meiktila for the delights of the YMCA in Calcutta. They tried opting for the YWCA, he says, but for some obscure reason the powers that be wouldn't allow it!!

But bereft of feminine company they soon got browned off visiting cinemas and eating out at Furpo's in the Charingi district, even though it was Calcutta's West End, and one outspoken type suggested they call it a day and head for Darjeeling instead, so grabbing kit bags etc. they boarded a train at Hara Station. From here to the base of the Himalayan foothills the track was conventional, after which to reach Darjeeling you journeyed on a narrower gauge.

'A truly fantastic journey,' says Ray, 'and if you needed to stretch your legs, all one had to do was jump train, clamber up the nearest hill and catch up with it on the next zigzag over on the opposite side.'

The train had climbed about 8,000 feet in order to reach Darjeeling, and with a temperature drop of two degrees Celsius every 1000 feet it would take a little while to acclimatise, on top of which the out on a limb journey meant no service unit was expecting them.

First duty as senior NCO, Ray searched out the RTO. This happened to be an army officer who listened but initially did not seem to digest their situation. The discourse went something akin to this:

The RTO: You shouldn't be here without a reservation! Where've you come from?

Ray: Calcutta but before that Mandalay!

(Now Mandalay when related to Darjeeling would seem like another world.)

The RTO: Mandalay!!!! You shouldn't be here! You should be at a rest camp!

Ray: Have you been to the rest camp?

(The conversation was clearly going nowhere. With the monsoons nearly on them and the rest camp in one of the wettest places in the world, you could often get over 200 inches of rain in a year.)

The RTO: It doesn't matter you still shouldn't be here. Where's your rail tickets?

Ray: Ooops! We don't have any, we just got on a train at Calcutta, and before that a Dakota at Mandalay!

The RTO was beginning to crumble, after more of the same he eventually decided enough was enough and reluctantly gave permission for all of them to stay in an empty house normally reserved for those who'd pre-booked accommodation was not forthcoming.

Talk about smelling of roses, the house in question had once belonged to a Hindu millionaire, and was quite modern compared to other palatial dwellings. From its vantage-point on the side of a hill it looked out directly towards the Himalayas which were constantly obscured by cloud. Here they all stayed for about a week enjoying not just the house and surroundings but the services of a bearer (manservant) who thoroughly cleaned their room every day. One or two crates of gin were laid on to see them safely through the nights, and most days Ray went horseriding.

An English lady who came to stay in an adjacent house with her daughter struck up a friendship with Ray and the lads she loved the fact they were all English and explained how they had come to Darjeeling to avoid the monsoons which were about to strike Calcutta.

They could made life very uncomfortable in that city and this was their retreat during the monsoon season; both her and her husband originally hailed from Northampton and he now acted as one of the superintendents in the Calcutta docks. As both she and Ray looked towards the distant horizon she observed that because of the expected arrival of the monsoons it was doubtful if they would ever see the eternal snows of the Himalayas. The clouds were very heavy and already the rains were late in coming.

Quite suddenly she let out a gasp: 'Oh look! You are lucky!' She was tugging at his arm. 'Look! There they are!'

Ray swung round staring intently at the horizon but could see nothing but cloud.

'No!' she exclaimed, 'not there at eye level, up there!' and she pointed almost straight up into the sky. Ray craned his neck back as far as he could and there they were way up in the sky, one long line of snow and ice covered peaks stretching as far as you could see, the sun bouncing off their tops, glistening and shimmering, a truly fantastic sight.

Right in the middle of the picture stood Mount Kanchenjunga, more than 28,000 feet high. Ray was having great difficulty in taking in the physical dimensions of the total scene. Almost six miles high and forty-five miles away as the crow flies, yet to walk it, many times that distance because of the row upon row of foothills in between. It was a sight that would live with him forever, how fortunate to have glimpsed the awesome spectacle just before they were due to leave.

As gin and time ran out, in corresponding order, so regretfully they retraced their steps. Firstly to Calcutta where the monsoons had now started. Then hitch-hiking a flight onwards to Chittagong before bedding down in a transit camp while Ray reconnoitred the airfield to ascertain their next transport to ferry them all to Mandalay.

Here, there were plenty of US Army Air Force Dakotas going through but most of them were full, however he did manage to extract one promise. Provided, he was told, he had his party available to board an aircraft at 6.00 am the following morning they would be airlifted. The best he could do to cover the journey in time to the field was obtain a Jeep that would need to travel the distance twice over.

Opting for the second run to make certain everybody was on time, Ray with just one other remaining clambered aboard and set off in the pitch dark and pouring rain. With nil visibility it wasn't long before there was one almighty bang and the occupants found themselves airborne. Clinging for dear life, somehow everyone managed to stay within the confines of the Jeep as unceremoniously it bounced back onto terra firma. With exclamations, not to mention four-letter words, emanating from everybody's lips, gingerly they extricated themselves to retrace their steps, peering anxiously see what the hell it was they'd hit.

As they inched forward, almost feeling their way in the darkness, slowly the obstruction emerged. 'I might have guessed,' croaked Ray, 'one of those damn sacred cows had lain sprawled bang in the centre of the road.' Well at least it had been until they hit it! Now as it staggered to its feet nobody was in the mood to ascertain what damage the beast had suffered, but hastily pushed on, thankful to be in one piece.

As luck would have it the slight delay hadn't destroyed his arrangements and sweeping into the field immediately they were directed towards a Dakota in the process of running both engines prior to take off at the far end of the runway. Pushed, pulled and cajoled by willing hands, both men found themselves aboard just as the US Army Air Force captain opened both throttles to send the Dak lumbering through the torrential rain and huge puddles lying across his path.

For a second Ray felt relief: 'Thank goodness,' he thought, 'this is the last leg of the journey.' Then slowly as his eyes became accustomed to the dimly lit interior he scanned along the fuselage to take in its occupants. Apart from his lads there must have been about twenty-four other types, but these were armed and wearing full battle kit, and every last one of them were huge, at least fourteen-stone, West Africans. 'But,' Ray is quick to remark, 'they were a terrific bunch and he'd never seen fighting men more happy.'

This flight would carry them over 7,000 feet mountains again but this time in monsoon weather. Unlike modern pressurised high flying aircraft the wartime Daks had to somehow negotiate the hazards as best they could, and whether it be fighter, transport or bomber, to fly these Eastern skies during such seasons demanded high skills and fortitude.

Quoting from a Special Correspondent report of the time I can give graphic indication from meteorological officers of the Eastern Air Command, and of RAF pilots who narrowly escaped with their lives from 'the devils playground' of the tropical skies.

The monsoon is now at its height, but flying goes on, and will go on throughout the season as in the past, though air operations may be held up from time to time. Experienced pilots in Burma are anxious that aircrews switching over from the European front should understand the hazards of monsoon flying.

Intense monsoon squalls with vertical currents whirling aloft at

100 miles per hour can tear the wings off a plane. The pilot sits helpless with controls icing, instruments useless through electrical disturbance, the aircraft a devils plaything tossed up and down, causing dangerous stresses, through torrential rain and hail.

Once a pilot has had personal experience of the monsoon he never flies into a squall unless he is forced to do it. I met one man however, who has done it twice, Sqdn. Ldr. A V D Taylor, an Australian, who with his navigator was commended four months ago for flying blind along the twisting valleys between the Arakan Mountains after his bomber had been damaged in an operation.

'I went into a monsoon squall the first time to see what it was like' he said, 'The second time I had to do it. That first time was the worst quarter of an hour of my life.

'I was flying a Liberator at 16,000ft over the Chin Hills when I met a dense black cloud towering 40,000ft. I would have had to go 30 miles round. I went in.

'The aircraft was thrown about violently. The compass went mad. All the instruments were haywire. By the airspeed indicator we were doing more than 200 miles an hour, but by the inclinometer we were going up 3,000ft a minute.

'Water streamed into the cockpit through the perspex joints like a forced feed spray. It was like hitting a wall of water. Lightning flashed along the wings and round the air-screw. I thought we would never escape alive. We came out at 9,000ft with the controls iced up.

'The second time I had to go into a monsoon because I had not enough fuel left to climb over the high mountains to the north. Though this squall was not so severe as the first, it took two of us all our time to hang on to the controls.'

Flt. Lt.Mickie Bryant, DFC of Bridgend, gave a similar account of monsoon phenomena.

I heard about an aircraft driven uncontrollably aloft while the pilot struggled in vain to push the stick forward, of five Spitfires that disappeared without a trace, of a Dakota that had a wing torn off, of a giant Sunderland flying boat that looped the loop, and of an aircraft, the pilot of which, finding himself getting weak noticed just in time that all his crew were unconscious. Flying blind through the monsoon with erratic instruments, he had unwittingly been forced to 30,000ft.

Daylight squalls are seen as formidable black cloud barriers 25 to 125 miles wide, but at night pilots often know only by the sudden violent bumping that they are heading for trouble.

Detailed advice on flying in the monsoon season is set out in meteorological notes for air crews at operational stations. Airmen are urged to make a study of tropical meteorology. They are told that there are three types of monsoon squall- the white, which can be flown through except at 12,000ft to 16,000ft, the black, which may be flown through at 100ft to 300ft; and the brown, the worst of all. It is suicide to fly into a brown squall.

Pilots are warned not to land in a squall, but keep clear until the short period of intensity is past. Faced with the deadly cumulonimbus, pilots must fly round it, turn back or else go underneath it at 100ft to 300ft.

Even this is not possible when the cloud comes down to ground level.

Most of this information Ray and his colleagues would have been blissfully unaware of as their Dakota bumped and creaked inexorably towards Mandalay. All Ray knew was that if they had to come down over such inhospitable territory they would be goners anyway, so why worry. He closed his eyes and fought hard to catch up on some lost sleep.

Looking back on his final triumphant arrival at Thedaw and rejoining of 152 Squadron, he rightly calculates that even in today's modern world of travel he'd still taken part in what would constitute a remarkable journey and one never to be easily forgotten.

All stops would now be pulled out to reach Rangoon, whatever else they must beat the Jap and the monsoon before things became so bad that they ground to a halt in the ever increasing mud.

Some ground staff, including Ray, were rushed further south to a place called Toungoo. Here they would service the squadron mainly with fuel and ammo so 152's Spits could assist in the advancing armies' operations. They worked non-stop for several days giving no respite to the tired and weary Japanese. Allied amphibian forces were now moving up from Rangoon and it was imperative that the forces met one another.

Unbeknown to all those at 152 both ground and air crews, the Japanese had pulled out of Rangoon and were beating a hasty retreat towards Thailand along almost the same route as the infamous Burma-Siam railway of death. Once news leaked out Ray couldn't help grimacing what poetic justice this was.

It was Douglas Cleverdon who had spent the first four months of 1945 in Burma as a BBC war correspondent who wrote the following dispatch for the Daily Telegraph at the conclusion of the campaign. I quote:

> *It is no disparagement of the troops who fought at Dunkirk, or in Normandy, or on the slopes of Monte Cassino to say that the toughest job in the last war was the Fourteenth Army's in Burma. Their commander, General Sir William Slim, described the Japanese as 'the most formidable fighting insects on earth'; and in the disastrous days of 1942, when the Japanese armies had captured Singapore and were swarming over the countries of the Far East, it was not surprising that a legend should grow up around the irresistible Jap superman, who could drop from the trees like a monkey and live in the jungle on a handful of rice a day.*
>
> *Of the fanatical bravery of the Japanese there was never any question. They literally preferred death to surrender. In the bitter fighting around Imphal and Kohima in 1944, when 50,000 died in battle or of starvation, fewer than 250 were taken prisoners—many of them because they were too severely wounded to avoid capture or suicide. A Japanese Order of the Day indeed actually instructed the Japanese soldier that if he was killed, that did not end his duty to his Emperor; his ghost must continue fighting.*
>
> *It was Lord Louis Mountbatten, as Supreme Commander of South East Asia Command, who first pricked the bubble of Japanese invincibility and reinforced the fighting spirit of the British troops by emphasising that 'intelligent free men can whip them every time'. But it was not only a human—or inhuman—enemy that the men of the Fourteenth Army had to contend with. As a theatre of war, Burma has nothing to recommend it. For six months of the year the monsoon rains deluge the country. In the worst parts the rainfall is 400 inches in six months; a normal rainfall in the hills is 200 inches compared with 27 inches in a twelvemonth in, say Manchester. As for the "hills" they range from 5,000 to 9,000 feet—twice the height of Snowdon—and run in knife-like ridges roughly from north to south.*

As the Fourteenth Army had to force its way back into Burma from the west to east, the campaign was fought up and down hillsides so steep, and so slippery in the blinding monsoon rains that on occasions even the pack-mules could not climb them and the loads had to be manhandled to the top. Then from the piercing cold of the hilltops, the fighting men would slither down to the steaming heat of the valleys, where jungle leeches and malaria, and—in the Kabaw Valley—the deadly scrub-typhus caused no less discomfort and danger than the Japanese themselves.

Never before in recorded history had an army fought through the monsoon; the Japanese had never planned to do so. In any case, they had expected to be victorious invaders of India before the monsoon started consequently, while the British troops were trained in anti-malarial discipline, the Japanese were caught on the wrong foot. Their supply system broke down, and they died in thousands from malaria and beri-beri. It was the turning point in the war.

By his daring decision to continue the campaign through the rains, Lord Louis Mountbatten had turned the monsoon into an ally.

The next stage—the advance through the central plain towards Mandalay—was by comparison a summer picnic. But after the fiercely contested crossing of the Irrawaddy and the capture of Mandalay, the pace quickened; for the only bridge across the mile-wide Irrawaddy had been blown up in 1942, and all supplies for the advancing Fourteenth Army had to be airborne.

It was essential to reach Rangoon within the next two months, before the start of the monsoon increased tenfold the difficulties of air supply.

The rains began a fortnight early; but thanks to a Combined Operation, Rangoon was ours and Burma with it.

Just a word about the men who fought this war!

Judged by their exploits, many of them might have been handpicked commandos—on Wingates expeditions, for instance, or on the shell-torn heights of Kohima, or the storming of Fort White, 9,000 feet up. But there was nothing handpicked about them. The British troops were largely infantrymen from the old country regiments. From India there came Hindus, Sikhs and Moslems, and Gurkhas from Nepal.

Birth of the Black Panthers

There were West Africans and East Africans.

In the north of Burma, Chinese divisions fought side by side with American volunteers—Merrill's Marauders'—under General Joe Stilwell. British and American pilots shared the hazards of the air-supply. And we should not forget the men from the loyal hill tribes of Burma—Nagas, Chins, Kachins, Karens and Lushis.

Among the graves of Kohima stands a memorial with this simple epitaph.

> When you go home,
> Tell them of us, and say
> "For your tomorrow"
> We gave our today".

On the sixth of August the Atom bomb was dropped on Hiroshima, and three days later, after the Japanese had refused to surrender, another destroyed the city of Nagasaki.

For Ray and 152 it spelt the end of the war, but they could always claim that although these terrible weapons brought hostilities to an end, they and everyone else involved had defeated the foe in Burma and won the country back before the nuclear devil entered the race.

TIME TO GO HOME

On the fifteenth of August V. J. "Victory over Japan" day Len wrote from Armarda Road to Sister Cecilia:

Whoohoo Ciss xxx

It's ended. Boy what a day this is to be in about 30 min's time.

Gee Wizz we were very near the point of juggling with old Jacob, saved by at least 5 min. [When studying his log book I can only imagine his reference to Jacob is because a bird crashed into his windscreen on 8th August entering the episode as dicey do. Airborne for only 15 minutes he obviously had to abort his exercise of squadron Skip Bomb to perform a quickie landing.]

Boy from now on I'm going to crawl around on my knees, standing up is too high. It shouldn't be long now Ciss before you see me. Let's hope Christmas "eh"

I'll come and sing Jingle Bells outside your door for 2d.

I hope Bill doesn't have to come out here now although I guess the kid is still keen to see the world. If he does your worries now aren't so much although I guess you still will "chump"

I feel so damned happy I want something to happen. I'm going to miss the good old Spit. Gee to think that old girl pulled me right through this war ever since 1941. The old girl kind of makes me feel sentimental and to quote poetry. Such as:

"Creed"
For all emotions that are tense and strong
And utmost knowledge I have lived for these
Lived deep and let the lesser things live long
The everlasting hills the lakes the trees
Who'd give their thousand years to sing this song

Birth of the Black Panthers

Of life and mans high sensibilities
Which I unto the face of death can sing
Oh death thou poor and disappointing thing.

Strike if thou wilt and soon strike breast and brow
For I have lived and thou can'st rob me now
Only of some long life that ne'er has been
The life that I have lived so full so keen
Is mine I hold it firm beneath thy blow
And dying take it with me where I go.

By the way Ciss I passed the exams ok.
So long for now Tally Ho
Give love to Rene, Elsie, etc my no 1 girl can have the most xxx Len.

(Len does not give any indication of the author of his favourite poem but there is little doubt its sentiment describe the way he viewed his life!)

The squadron without the aircraft moved down to Mingladon, an airfield near Rangoon, whilst their flying fraternity took the Spits to an airstrip at Zayatkwin. Arriving on the 20th August 1945 they began to drop leaflets over the Imperial Japanese Army, informing them that the war was definitely over. These were carried on the Spits' flaps, which were then lowered, releasing the leaflets at the appropriate time.

Obviously the leaflets were in Japanese, but to make certain nothing could be misconstrued, on the reverse side, a photograph showing the Japanese surrender party arriving in Rangoon had been printed. No. 152 had actually been given the honour of escorting the Japanese party into Rangoon, but as bad luck would have it, the Japanese were running late that day, and with fuel reaching dangerous levels they were forced to hand over to another squadron.

With the fighting over, the men wandered aimlessly, Ray sensed the strangest of feelings, as though everything was held in suspension, at a standstill, all of a sudden there was no urgency and very little to occupy the mind.

Gradually new orders seeped through. They were going to form part of the occupying forces, although having absorbed this, immediately confusion reigned with instructions being countermanded as quickly as they were issued. Firstly they were all going to Bangkok, or was it Saigon? It was Bangkok, well at least Ray and a few others were being flown to Bangkok under the command of their engineering officer, but unbeknown to them all the Spits were to go to Tengah and the remaining ground crews airlifted to Saigon. Ray's group was to join everyone within six weeks. In the interim they would help service and refuel other Spits at Don Muaung Airport, Bangkok.

Trouble was that all transport aircraft travelling eastward from Bangkok were constantly full and any thoughts of an early reunion with 152 began to fade: in the event, complained Ray, they never did qualify as a complete squadron again despite reaching Saigon just before his repatriation.[8]

Life during their stay at Bangkok threw up some odd aspects, often they had joked over the previous two years about the possibility of one day having to operate from the opposite end of the same airfield as the Nips. Here at Bangkok they went one better with their ex-enemies utilising the same hangar.

Having command of their own Jeep, Flt Sgt Flash Fenton and Ray would often make sorties into the city, where as yet few occupying troops had been established. This gave opportunity for the two NCOs to have a fairly free run when visiting local nightspots, where one in particular sported the chief of Bangkok's police. Here, they wasted little time in softening him up with English cigarettes, and both were treated and felt like rulers of the Royal Air Force.

One big drawback appeared to be the local whiskey, which as it transpired, turned out to be the only alcoholic beverage available. Known as Black and White its labelled trademark showed not the usual pair of Scottie dogs denoting the pure and prestigious Scottish blend, but ominous looking cats. Ray and the lads were quite convinced that this exterior image held a strong affinity to its interior contents.

---

8 Actually on the 11th September the Spits flew to Penang (Kallang) staying there a short time before flying on to Tengah (Singapore) and remaining there until disbandment on March 10th 1946. But life for 152 was not to end so abruptly because on the 8th May that same year they would be taken over by No. 136 Squadron after that squadron lost its number and became 152 instead during transit to Worli and began flying Spitfires again in early June whilst awaiting arrival of their Tempests. Unfortunately when they did get them during the first week of August the spares situation was so grim little flying activity could be accomplished and by 15th January the following year 152 would again be disbanded with their current complement of aircraft being handed over to No. 5 Squadron.

It wouldn't be until June 1st 1954 that 152 again reared its head, being reformed at Wattisham, only this time with Meteor jets operating as night fighters to form part of the UK air defence. This latest deployment would last until 31st July 1958 when 152 again found itself disbanded. However like the boxer who wouldn't stay down 152 reared its head for the final time when provided with Percival Pembroke and Twin Pioneer transport aircraft from 1417 squadron. They continued to operate these from Bahrain until their sad demise on the 9th December 1967.

Jack was Ciss's husband and his character is described in greater detail in my memoir, *The Way We Were*.

Birth of the Black Panthers

Service drinking water at this time had been heavily chlorinated, a fact that didn't encourage dilution of the whiskey. As a consequence it wasn't long before types became ill, with the engineering officer the first to fall foul of something or other, quickly followed by Ray experiencing a high temperature before rising one morning coupled with excruciating pains in the small of his back. Blocked kidneys, diagnosed the MO, giving him a horrible-looking mixture to swallow and advising a large intake of the chlorinated water he'd previously been loath to partake of.

During this early period of occupation there seemed to be more Japanese in the area than Allied forces, sometimes they were even conscripted to do guard duty utilising their own weapons. Ray felt nauseated by the way they were constantly bowing and scraping as if trying to ingratiate themselves, but the lads were inclined to ignore them, only making contact through an interpreter whenever a menial task was called for.

A particular Spitfire squadron passing through at this time may have been fairly new to their machines, because a couple were pranged coming in to land. This episode afforded a good opportunity to badger the Japanese into some heavy work manhandling the damaged Spits a few hundred yards clear of the runway and towards the hangars.

'Afterwards,' says Ray, 'you could see them huddled in a group chatting amongst themselves and looking furtively towards the RAF ground crews.' He couldn't help grinning and wondered what the Nipponese words for 'rotten bastards' might have been.

At the cessation of hostilities the powers that be had decided in their wisdom to change the format of the squadron organisation. From this moment on the air component would keep the designate number, but ground crew would receive a prefix number. Thus, 152 ground crew would be known henceforth as 7-152 Servicing Echelon.

Such a dictum of course did little for morale, to divorce the ground element from their air personnel was tantamount to destroying the close relationship the squadron had previously enjoyed. Needless to say the whole rigmarole was totally ignored by squadron commanders downward during this difficult phase.

Group Captain Donald Finlay (a former Olympic athlete) was drafted in to form HQ Siam from SEAC, and shortly after this Ray's detachment was forwarded to the airfield at Saigon. His homeward journey was now very near, but before bidding farewell to squadron life and the Far East forever, he was able to witness the final humiliation with the symbolic laying down of arms in total surrender of the Imperial Japanese Forces.

Mountbatten had insisted that the ceremonial samurai sword be used, and Field Marshal Count Tourochi, the Japanese C-in-C, was forced to dispatch his aide to Tokyo to retrieve one; in the event two were brought and duly handed over.

At the time rumours circulated that General MacArthur was unhappy at any prior ceremonies taking place before the main surrender at Tokyo Bay, but Lord Louis and the British managed to have their day.

On tenth November 1945 Len wrote from Peshawar to Sister Ciss:

Hello precious,

I guess its about time I wrote to you what a bad lad I am but I'm damned if I can find time to write I'm either playing hockey, football or rugby – swimming ? too cold Brrrrr.

I bet your getting ready for Christmas, pull a cracker for me, its too bad I can't be there but you'll bet your life I'll have a wizo time – I have a cute little Q.A.sister to run around with, six nights a week now I see her not bad eh?

Here's some real gen for you – I've now got myself a wizo job Test Pilot every day up to 30,000 feet and wiffle sniffle down again it's the last word believe me. When I'm not flying I get stuck into one of the engines just to see what makes the fan go round, Jack would love it I know.

I'm the only one doing it here so at the present I am my own boss except the C.T.O. who's the chief technical officer – a non flying type he's the gen for he hopes to get my F/LT through as this is a flight lieut's job.

I'm doing it for I have over 1000hrs in now and trying to get 1000 on Spits alone.

I should do it easy before I get home [Why] I've heard there's a Test Pilots course   in England. If I make good here and with those hours I should stand a chance. I hope, I hope, I hope.

Well papers short so you've had it.

So long Ciss, bags of love. Len

x Gooey kiss

P.S. A Merry Christmas pal xxx

Birth of the Black Panthers

Len wrote Sister Cecilia the following year to explain in his own inimitable way his explanation of the phrase *wiffle sniffle*.

All I do is go downwards like the wiffle sniffle bird. You know what the wiffle sniffle bird is? Well it's a little bird that climbs and climbs into the ethereal blue where its wings will ne'er support it, thereupon it puts its nose earthwards crying wiffle sniffle, wiffle sniffle. – Which to you or I means nothing, "But" to the little bird means Christ! What a sensation! What a sensation. Quite a little bird isn't it!

By early November Ray bid adieu to the wide boulevards and roadside estaminets reminiscent of France in the beautiful old city of Saigon and boarded a Dakota to start his long and tedious journey home. First to Bangkok, then Rangoon and on to Mandalay, Chittagong and Calcutta. Pushed into a transit camp he quickly learnt that he was to be entrained for Bombay, a hideous journey. So without further ado arranged his own flight onward managing to land somewhere near the city. What precise airfield he was unsure, thankful only to have avoided the monotonous rail trek.

Because all British armed forces fighting throughout India and Burma paid their taxes to the Indian Inland Revenue, clearance had to be sought at Bombay to make doubly sure no defaulters tried to escape. Fortunately Ray's papers seemed to be in order so laden with his kit bag and any otherworldly possessions he'd managed to accumulate he dragged himself up the gangplank of the illustrious liner, the SS *Île de France* to set sail for the Cape of Good Hope.

This French ship had been purposely built for the North Atlantic run, and was therefore much too large to circumnavigate the Suez Canal which meant the final leg of their journey home would have to be via the Cape with a stopover at Durban. She was also inclined to roll a lot in the heavy seas and weather experienced in these southern latitudes, though Ray did say, seasickness among those aboard seemed not to be a problem.

Although their French galley crews believed they could have provided better for these homeward bound heroes, the general consensus was they had been done proud and there was certainly no room for complaint.

Christmas 1945 was spent at sea quite near the Equator and hardly Santa Claus weather, where soon afterwards they hove to at Freetown to take on much needed water.

Then quietly on a chill January day in 1946 the *Île de France* slid into Southampton water and began to disgorge its mass of uniformed personnel for entraining onwards to their various demobilisation centres. Ray's particular venue was Hennesford, from where he phoned home to advise his folks of his impending visit. The call came as quite a shock, for neither his mother nor father had the remotest idea he was back in the old country.

He learnt afterwards that, having spoken only to his father at work, his dad never let on immediately to his mother but kept her guessing as to who that day he had been speaking to! As his RAF career came to an end and their prodigal son finally stepped over the threshold Ray liked to think they were both thrilled! 'I'm sure they were,' he wrote.

And brother Len! Smithy returned to our shores in July 1946, a full Flight Lieutenant to be posted as Officer Commanding B Flight No. 237 Squadron, currently acting as No. 8 Operational Training Unit from Chalgrove in Oxfordshire.

From here I saw him after my own return from abroad lead the Battle of Britain display in September 1947 flying a clipped wing Mark XVI Spitfire. In April 1948 the unit moved to Leuchars in Fife, Scotland, while across the bay stood the Royal and Ancient Burgh of St Andrews. A Scottish lass from the university town became Smithy's love and they both agreed to the banns being called after the 1948 Battle of Britain display in which he would again lead.

Unfortunately a fellow officer whilst flying Len's favourite Mark XVI suffered a glycol leak which having spewed the liquid over the Spitty's windscreen, caused the pilot to land heavily, resulting in the plane being taken out of commission. Undaunted Len asked his C/O, Sqn Ldr B Lover DFC if he could take one of the Mark XIX photo-reconnaissance Spitfires for display instead, to which his C/O readily agreed. The plane in question was one he had flown several times before and with which he was well acquainted.

On the day as Smithy pulled the plane into what would be a rocket loop from a height of only 300 feet, above his fiancée's head, so immediately it began to belch black smoke and then quickly break up. First the port wing folded back, striking the tail which in turn disintegrated leaving the bulk of the remainder to crash at over 400 mph into a wood on the far side of the airfield.

The tragedy made headline news and Mary, who had seen it all, felt compelled to travel south with the coffin to our home, accompanied by a couple of his fellow officers. We met for the very first time, and after further invited visits over Christmas and beyond, we fell in love and married in the following spring.

In April 1999 we celebrated our golden anniversary with our two sons Teri and Barry, and our six grandchildren. And to end on an even happier note, Teri is Smithy's son, and the spitting image of Len despite his current fifty-two years.

Epilogue

Some years ago I came across "The Funeral Oration spoken by PERICLES in 429 B.C." and feel that his words uttered so long ago also pay tribute to our comrades who never returned. I also believe it is a fitting finale to this brief history of No 152 (Hyderabad) Squadron, R.A.F.

Each one, man for man, has won imperishable praise, each one has gained a glorious grave, not that sepulchre of earth wherein they lie, but the living tomb of everlasting rememberance wherein their glory is enshrined.

For the whole earth is the sepulchre of heroes, monuments may rise and tablets be set up to them in their own land, but on the far-off shores is an abiding memorial that no pen or chisel has traced.

It is given, not on stone or brass, but on the heart of humanity.

Take these men for your example, like them, remember that prosperity can only be for the free: that freedom is the pure possession of those who have the courage to defend it.

Roy Johnson
November 2001

1943 - Len's Log showing flight of new MK VIII Spits from Helwan, Egypt to Baigachi, India

These Spits had their Cannon & Ammo. removed to enable pilots to stow their gear

YEAR 1943 MONTH / DATE		AIRCRAFT Type	No.	PILOT, OR 1ST PILOT	2ND PILOT, PUPIL OR PASSENGER	DUTY (INCLUDING RESULTS AND REMARKS)
—	—	—	—	—	—	— TOTALS BROUGHT FORWARD
				CIARO	EGYPT	
Nov	26	SPITFIRE VIII	JF522	SELF		HELWAN To CIARO WEST
Nov	27	SPITFIRE VIII	JF522	SELF		CIARO WEST To RAFFH
Nov	28	SPITFIRE VIII	JF522	SELF		RAFFH To H 3
Nov	27	SPITFIRE VIII	JF522	SELF		H 3 To HABBANIYH
Nov	28	SPITFIRE VIII	JF522	SELF		HABBANIYH To SHAIBAH
Nov	28	SPITFIRE VIII	JF522	SELF		SHAIBAH To BAHREIN ISLAND
Nov	29	SPITFIRE VIII	JF522	SELF		FORCE LANDED
Nov	30	SPITFIRE VIII	JF522	SELF		BAHREIN ISLAND To SHARJAH
Nov	30	SPITFIRE VIII	JF522	SELF		SHARJAH To JAWANI
Nov	30	SPITFIRE VIII	JF522	SELF		JAWANI To MARIPUR INDIA
				SUMMARY FOR OCT + NOV 1943		1 SPITFIRE MONTH
				SQUADRON 152(?)		2 SPITFIRE TOTAL
				DATE 1:12:1943		3 SPITFIRE TOTAL OPS
				SIGNATURE		4
Dec	14	SPITFIRE VIII	JF522	SELF		MARIPUR To JODHPUR
Dec	14	SPITFIRE VIII	JF522	SELF		JODHPUR To DELHI
Dec	14	SPITFIRE VIII	JF522	SELF		DELHI To ALLAHABAD
Dec	15	SPITFIRE VIII	JF522	SELF		ALLAHABAD To GAYA
Dec	15	SPITFIRE VIII	JF522	SELF		GAYA To BAIGACHI
Dec	18	SPITFIRE VIII	M	SELF		BAIGACHI To ALIPORE
Dec	18	SPITFIRE VIII	M	SELF		ALIPORE To BAIGACHI

GRAND TOTAL [Cols. (1) to (10)]
559 Hrs. 20 Mins.
TOTALS CARRIED FORWARD

Flight to India, 1943

1943 - Continuation of Len's Log showing flight times and comments on the journey to Baigachi

SINGLE-ENGINE AIRCRAFT				MULTI-ENGINE AIRCRAFT						PASS-ENGER	INSTR./CLOUD FLYING [Incl. in cols. (1) to (10)]	
DAY		NIGHT		DAY			NIGHT					
DUAL	PILOT	DUAL	PILOT	DUAL	1ST PILOT	2ND PILOT	DUAL	1ST PILOT	2ND PILOT		DUAL	PILOT
(1)	(2)	(3)	(4)	(5)	(6)	(7)	(8)	(9)	(10)	(11)	(12)	(13)
63·35	446·30	3·55	20·30	8·45						2·10	18·10	12·45
	·30					SET OUT FROM CAIRO NOTHING BUT SAND						
	1·20											
	1·30					H3 STUCK OUT IN MIDDLE OF SAND						
	1·00											
	1·35											
	1·40					A WIZARD ISLAND DIAMONDS DIVED FOR HERE						
	·20					OVER LOAD CABLE SAME AWAY						
	1·50					PICKED UP SECOND CONVOY						
	1·55					JAWANI VISAY BRO MEALS POOR SHOW						
	1·35					MADE IT WITH A GLYCOL LEAK						
	18·35											
	394:55											
	188:15											
				O.C. 152 Sqd		½ of flight		Sgt	½			
	1·45											
	1·25											
	1·20											
	1·10											
	1·40											
	·15											
	·15											
63·35	4035	3·55	20·30	8·45						2·10	18·10	12·45
(1)	(2)	(3)	(4)	(5)	(6)	(7)	(8)	(9)	(10)	(11)	(12)	(13)

Flight from Egypt to India

SINGLE-ENGINE AIRCRAFT				MULTI-ENGINE AIRCRAFT						PASS-ENGER	INSTR./CLOUD FLYING (Incl. in cols. (1) to (10))	
DAY		NIGHT		DAY			NIGHT					
DUAL	PILOT	DUAL	PILOT	DUAL	1ST PILOT	2ND PILOT	DUAL	1ST PILOT	2ND PILOT		DUAL	PILOT
(1)	(2)	(3)	(4)	(5)	(6)	(7)	(8)	(9)	(10)	(11)	(12)	(13)
63·35	467·35	3·55	20·30	3·45						2·10	18·10	12·45
1·10												
1·20												
·55				VALIOMO OILO B/O NO LUCK %MCDONALD & %PATTERSON								
1·05				SHOT DOWN %IN FLAMES %/A (OILED)								
1·20												
12·40												
409·35												
199·10												
				O.C. 152 Sqn. _____ %/2 O.C. FLIGHT _____ %/2								
1·10												
1·05												
·10												
·50												
·30												
1·00				SGT COLE CRASHED THROUGH LACK OF OXYGEN — KILLED								
1·30												
·30												
·15												
·50												
·25												
63·35	482·40	3·55	20·30	3·45						2·10	18·10	12·45
(1)	(2)	(3)	(4)	(5)	(6)	(7)	(8)	(9)	(10)	(11)	(12)	(13)

Len's log records loss of Sgt. Cole

1944 - Chittagong

Len's log from March 2nd to 19th

Baigachi, India - 1943

NO. 152 (HYDERABAD) SQUADRON.

COMMANDING OFFICER - S/Ldr. M.R.B. INGRAM, D.F.C.   1.
DEPUTY COMMANDING OFFICER - Capt. W.H. HOFFE.

"A" Flight.   "B" Flight.

Flight Commander - F/Lt. Jones, D.F.C. 2,   Flight Commander - Capt. W.H. Hoffe. 3.
Deputy   "   "   - F/O. Allington. 4,   Deputy "   "   - F/O. Bell.   5.
                    F/O. Bissett.   6.   F/O. MacDonald.   7.
                    F/O. Dobson.   8.   F/O. King.   9.
                    Lt. Peirce.   18.   Lt. Potgeiter.   17.
                    Lt. Croad.   Lt. Haynes.

Senior Sgts.   F/Sgt. Smith.   10.   Senior Sgts. F/Sgt. Patterson.   11.
                    F/Sgt. Dear.   12.   F/Sgt. Southward.   13.
                    Sgt. Eels.   14.   Sgt. Whittling.   15.
                    F/Sgt. O'Grady. 16,   Sgt. Bray.   19.
                    F/Sgt. Turner. 29.   Sgt. Pappa.
                    Sgt. Berry.   Sgt. Cobley.
                                                           F/Sgt. Forbes.

Squadron Senior N.C.O. Pilot - F/Sgt. Smith.

Flying compliment

P/O Cobley   W/O Turner   F/Sgt Berry

India 1943/44

A Flight football team

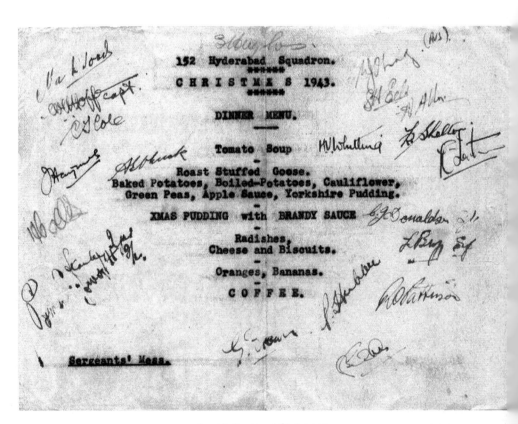

A well deserved Christmas

Imphal Box - June 1944

152 line up at Padel - Imphal's most southern strip

Slightly battle weary, but still fighting fit

Gus Ardeline   Len   Eric Clegg
Pilots of 152 Squadron inside the Imphal Box.

Laying to rest of one of the greatest men Smithy ever knew.
Goodbye S/Ldr Bruce Ingram DFC, RMZAF.
Well loved c/O of 152 Squd.

S/Ldr Bruce Ingram DFC laid to rest

Tulihall, India - October 1944

Ye Olde Nogg Inne and best Spit
Sgt's mess "unfortunately without Ray"
Left to Right: Clegg, Denny, Duval, Orderly, Bell, Jimmy, Reg, Black, Vickers, Cousins,
Bluey, Ron Partridge - Unsworth in front

Best little Spit in the business

November - Jungle accommodation

Spitfire Screen

Pilot protection

Black Panther's are born

Panther's in a row:
Ron Partridge, Jock, The Black Cat, Vicky, Paddy Foser

Panther's at Dispersal "Somewhere in Burma"

Entry to Burma - November 1044

There's the sign - Now all we have to do is make the road

The Four Musketeer's Four Musketeers and Burma border
Vicky, Len, Unsworth and Paddy Foster

1944 - Tamu, Burma

SINGLE-ENGINE AIRCRAFT				MULTI-ENGINE AIRCRAFT						PASS-ENGER	INSTR./CLOUD FLYING [incl. in cols. (1) to (10)]	
DAY		NIGHT		DAY			NIGHT					
DUAL	PILOT	DUAL	PILOT	DUAL	1ST PILOT	2ND PILOT	DUAL	1ST PILOT	2ND PILOT		DUAL	PILOT
(1)	(2)	(3)	(4)	(5)	(6)	(7)	(8)	(9)	(10)	(11)	(12)	(13)
63·35	585·45	3·55	21·05	8·45						2·10	18·10	12·45
	·30			WIZARD FLYING AGAIN								
	2·00			SHOT UP RAILWAY TRUCK ALSO LARGE SAMPANS								
	2·00			KILLED TWO JAPS AND TWO PROB STRAFFED SAMPANS								
	1·45			ANOTHER JAP BIT THE DUST								
	·35											
	6·50											
	615·30											
	272·50											
				O. C. 152 Sqdn [signature] MAJR O.C 'A' FLIGHT [signature]								
	1·45			NOTHING SEEN								
	1·00											
	1·50			STRAFFED GUN POS. STEAM ROLLER AND RAILWAY TRUCKS								
	·45			MIXED IT WITH 12 PLOS ZERO'S DES ONE DAM ONE								
	2·00			F/LT JONES GOT PROB VIZO SCRAP								
	·55			NOTHING SEEN								
	2·00											
	1·45											
	2·00											
	1·10			NO LUCK								
	1·55											
63·35	607·40	3·55	21·05	8·45						2·10	18·10	12·45

Len's Log - October 20th to November 13th
November 5th Len's log claims one Zero destroyed and one damaged

Len and Charlie at the charge

Dawn scramble captured by Len

Christian Names: Leonard, Alfred.   Surname: SMITH.

Rank: Flight Sergeant.   Number: 1376329   Group: 221

Unit: No. 152 (HYDERABAD) Squadron, Royal Air Force.

Appointment held or how employed.   PILOT. (Section Leader)

PARTICULARS OF MERITORIOUS SERVICE.

This pilot possesses an exceptional keenness to carry out his duties and always shown amazing tenacity when operating against the Enemy. The 4½ aircraft he destroyed while covering the advance of the First Army were the result of his determination to frustrate the Enemy and of his skill and courage which enabled him to press home his attacks. Whilst operating in this Command his efforts and keeness have been maintained and he has destroyed two (2) Barges, Four (4) Motor Launches and ten (10) Motor Transports. He is a most reliable N.C.O. whose coolness, cheerfulness and bravery under difficult conditions are an inspiration to his brother pilots and ground crews.

Recognition recommended.   DISTINGUISHED FLYING MEDAL.

Dtd: 26th August, 1944.   (signed.) ~~~~~~~~~ Major.
                              Officer Commanding,
                              No. 152 (Hyderabad) Squadron.

HEADQUARTERS   221 GROUP ROYAL AIR FORCE.

DO/SFV/1/377

22nd January, 1945.

Dear Smith,

        Many congratulations on the award of the D.F.M. which has come through this morning.

        It is very good news, and you can join the comparatively few who have the honour to wear the D.F.M., as so many either reach Warrant rank or get commissioned and, therefore, get the D.F.C., and in my opinion the D.F.M. is worth more than the D.F.C. as there are definitely, partly for the above reason, far fewer per hundred N.C.O. pilots with the D.F.M. than there are Officer pilots with the D.F.C. and, therefore, one has to get the D.F.M. quicker. (Rather a tangled sentence, I find, on reading through!)

        Wishing you the best of luck.

                          Yours sincerely,

                          S.F. Vincent.

F/O L. Smith, D.F.M.,
No. 152 Squadron.

Len becomes 152's first and possibly only DFM.
Certainly I have been unable to locate any other.

F/Lt. S. Tyas,
No. 907 Wing,
Royal Air Force,
India.

29th January, 1945.

Dear Len,

Immediately I arrived upon No. 152 Squadron, I knew that "Smithy" was something out of the ordinary and quite a character. Now "Smithy" is commissioned and decorated. Good old "Smithy". I feel honoured Len to have played some small part in your life and I am exceptionally delighted to hear of your decoration. You deserve it old fellow, every bit of it.

You started at the bottom and by sheer grit and determination, in addition to flying ability, you are gradually working your way up the Ladder of Success and in closing I can only say "Congratulations, good health, and good hunting in the air above 1,000 ft.

Your sincere friend,

F/Lt Stan Tyas, I feel sure was one time Adjutant of 152 Sqdn.

February 13th, 1945 - Airfield attacked

Damaged Panthers

Len surveys the work of one nasty Nip

Jungle types - Vicky as Tarzan and Head-hunter

Vicky as me! Tarzan

A real Head-shrinker

152 squadron Harvard

India – Calcutta – Vicky and Len on grog run

Mountbatten telegram

SOUTH EAST ASIA COMMAND HEADQUARTERS.

25th February, 1945

My dear Kerr,

       I am very grateful to you and your Squadron for providing fighter cover for me when I was down in your Area recently, and I shall be most grateful if you would pass on a special word of thanks to Flying Officer Smith and other pilots who flew with him.

       I am afraid that our rendezvous in the early hours of the morning did not come off, but that was entirely because we were several minutes ahead of schedule.

       You and the other Squadrons in your Area certainly seem to be on top of the Jap these days, as whenever I hear that enemy aircraft have been up over our lines you seem to dispose of about half their number.

       Good luck to you.

       Yours sincerely,

       LOUIS MOUNTBATTEN.

P.S. Tell my friend Vickers that I will see him in Futo's some day

L.M.
(Dook)

This copy of Mountbatten's telegram passed to Len by F/O "Dook" Allington, who whilst at Baigachi held the position of Deputy Command "A" Flight

Burma bathing

Bathing Burma style

Jungle refueling

YEAR 1945		AIRCRAFT		PILOT, OR 1ST PILOT	2ND PILOT, PUPIL OR PASSENGER	DUTY (INCLUDING RESULTS AND REMARKS)
MONTH	DATE	Type	No.			
—	—	—	—	—	—	—— TOTALS BROUGHT FORWARD
MARCH	29	SPITFIRE VIII	M	SELF		MONYWA & BACK
MARCH	30	SPITFIRE VIII	K	SELF		PATROL PAGAN
		SUMMARY		FOR MARCH 1945	1.	SPITFIRE MONTH
		SQUADRON		152 (F)	2.	SPITFIRE TOTAL
		DATE		31 · 3 · 45	3.	SPITFIRE TOTAL OPS
		SIGNATURE		_LSt_ 70	4.	

SUMMARY of FLYING and ASSESSMENTS ON 19

	S.E. AIRCRAFT.		M.E. AIRCRAFT.		TOTAL for year	GRAND TOTAL All Service flying.
	Day	Night.	Day	Night.		
DUAL	63·35	3·55	8·45			76·15
PILOT	800·35	21·05			122·45	821·40
PASSENGER						

===

ASSESSMENT of ABILITY. (To be assessed as: Exceptional, Above the Average, Average, or Below the Average).

    (i) AS A FIGHTER PILOT.... _Above the Average_

    (ii) AS PILOT-NAVIGATOR/NAVIGATOR.... _Above the Average_

    (iii) IN BOMBING.... _N.A._

    (iv) IN AIR GUNNERY.... _Above the Average_

+ Insert "F", "L.B", "G.R", "F. B", etc.

===

ANY POINTS IN FLYING OR AIRMANSHIP WHICH SHOULD BE WATCHED.

........................_Nil_........................

===

Signature..... _Grant Kerr S/L_

Date.............. Officer Commanding. 152 HYDERABAD SQDN.

GRAND TOTAL [Cols. (1) to (10)]

.....897....Hrs.......55....Mins.

TOTALS CARRIED FORWARD

1945, March 30th

S/Ldr Grant Kerr gives his assessment as Len leaves 152 Sqd

SINGLE-ENGINE AIRCRAFT				MULTI-ENGINE AIRCRAFT						PASS-ENGER	INSTR/CLOUD FLYING [incl. in cols. (1) to (10)]	
DAY		NIGHT			DAY			NIGHT				
DUAL	PILOT	DUAL	PILOT	DUAL	1ST PILOT	2ND PILOT	DUAL	1ST PILOT	2ND PILOT		DUAL	PILOT
(1)	(2)	(3)	(4)	(5)	(6)	(7)	(8)	(9)	(10)	(11)	(12)	(13)
63·35	798·10	3·55	21·05	8·45						2·10	18·10	12·45
	·40											
	1·45											
	34·25											
	735·30											
	470·45											

O.C. 142 Squn. ......*G.Vet.*......... ⅌.   O.C. "A"Flight ......*J. Smith*...... ⅌.

O.F.C.

*G.day bye. Smith. Thank you for everything you have
done for our Squadron. All the very best in your
future undertakings. We are all sorry to see you go.*

Garry Vett

⅌.

63·35	798·10	3·55	21·05	8·45						2·10	18·10	12·45
	800·35											
(1)	(2)	(3)	(4)	(5)	(6)	(7)	(8)	(9)	(10)	(11)	(12)	(13)

Goodbye from Gary

```
— ENGLAND. —                          165 Sqdn
Oct 8th 1942 to Nov 2nd  (GRAVESEND) & (TANGMERE)      15 SORTIES      OPS  18.20
Nov 2nd  "   to Jan 13th

— NORTH AFRICA —                      152 Sqdn
Feb 16 1943 to March 12  (SOUK 'EL' KHEMIS)           44 SORTIES      OPS  38       CAT  MAD  DM
                 May 13                                                             ME 109G  ?

— NORTH AFRICA —
May 13 1943 to May 19  (PROTVILLE)                     5 SORTIES      OPS  4.05   —   —   —

— MALTA —
June 13 1943 to July 20  (TA KALI)                    23 SORTIES      OPS  25.15  1½  —
                                                                                   REGGIANE 2001.

— SICILY —
July 21 1943 to Sept 5  (LENTINI)                     31 SORTIES      OPS  40.05   1   —    —
                                                                                   ME 109E

— SICILY —
Sept 6 1943 to Sept 16  (MILAZZO)                     12 SORTIES      OPS  27.25   —   —    —

— ITALY —
Sept 16 1943 to Sept 23  (ASA)                         9 SORTIES      OPS  15.00   1   —    1
                                                                                   FW190      FW190

— ITALY —
Sept 23 1943 to Oct 13  (SERRETELLA)                   2 SORTIES      OPS  2.25

— ITALY —
Oct 13 1943 to Nov 3  (GIOIA)                          2 SORTIES      OPS  2.20

— CAIRO —   — INDIA
Nov 26 1943 to Dec 18  (HELWAN) (AMIGACHI)

— INDIA —
Dec 18 1943 to Feb 21 1944  (AMIGACHI)                 6 SORTIES      OPS  4.45

— INDIA —
Feb 21 1944 to March 25  (DOUBLE MOORING)              7 SORTIES      OPS  8.25    —   —

— INDIA —
March 25 1944 to May 1  (CHITTAGONG)                   8 SORTIES      OPS  11.25   —   —

— INDIA —
May 1 1944 to June 17  (CAMILLA)                        2 SORTIES      OPS  2.55

— INDIA —
June 17 1944 to Oct 29  (IMPHAL)                       35 SORTIES      OPS  58.20   —   —

— BURMA —
Oct 29 1944 to Jan 15 1945  (MHAN)(TAMU)               63 SORTIES      OPS  96.45   1   —    1
                                                                                   ZERO       ZER?

— BURMA —
Jan 15 1945 to Feb 7  (KAN)                            17 SORTIES      OPS  30.35

— BURMA —
Feb 7 1945 to March 30  (SINTHE)                       42 SORTIES      OPS  76.10   —   —    —
                                     CLAIMS
A/C IN AIR      A/C DECK        SHIPS                 TRUCKS        SAMPANS
 6½ DES          2 DES    OIL TANKER 1 DAM            25 DES         18 DES
                         MOTOR LAUNCH 4 DES
```

Len's record in his own hand

LEN PORTRAIT
F/LT LEONARD ALFRED "SMITHY" SMITH, DFM
14-04-20 TO 18-09-48

152 SQUADRON
16TH MARCH '43 TO 30TH MARCH '45

Mr Ian Stephens, Editor - The Statesman - India

The Statesman LTD.

STATESMAN HOUSE

Our Ref.......................... Calcutta, January 21, 1946.

Dear Mr.Smith,

I am asked by Mr.Ian Stephens to say that he expects to proceed to England on leave towards the end of the first week of February and to return to India at the end of next July.

Should you be in England about the same time, Mr.Stephens says it would be nice to meet you there.

Mr.Stephens is at the moment in Rangoon on a brief visit to Burma at the invitation of the Governor Sir Reginald Dorman-Smith. He hopes to write to you before he leaves for England.

Yours sincerely,

H. Maidment

(H.Maidment)
P.A. to the Editor.

F/O Smith, DFM,
151 O.T.U.,
R.A.F.Station,
Peshawar,
SEAAF.

Ian Steven's PA writes to Len

This postcard is to sister Cecilia "Ciss" an dated 20th February 1946. It reads:

Earls Court Hotel, Tunbridge Wells
Many thanks for your kind letter much appreciated. I'm glad Smithy gave me good testimonial. Bad business he's not back yet. could you please let me have his present Indian address, there seems possibility my still being around if he's back in April, and I very much like to avil myself of the kind invitation from you and your husband. It would be fun to meet you about whom he's told me, and to see the great man fresh from the tropics in your midst. Best wishes meanwhile.
Yours, Ian Stephens

This card brings to you, from IAN STEPHENS, his Kindliest remembrances, the Compliments of the Season, and Cordial Good Wishes for Your Happiness in 1947

This card arrived from Ian at Christmas, 1947

August – Japanese Unconditional Surrender Leaflet
These leaflets picturing the High Command on one side and surrender messgae on the other, were carried inside the Spitfire flap area, so when opened they would automatically disperse exactly where the pilots wished them to.

号外

南方軍總司令官陸軍大將
内伯爵ノ命ニヨリ
長沼田中將ハ日本軍緬甸旬參
退準備打合セノ日本軍緬甸旬
六日蘭貢ニ到着セリ八月二
真八總參謀長沼田中將及
聯合軍幹部將校ナリ

号外

緬甸方面軍司令官木村中將ハ
入エゲイン―パアブン線上ニ
南方ノ日本軍ニ對シ休戰命
下達濟ノ旨聯合軍總司令官ニ
通報セリ猶本村中將ハ同聯
合軍總司令官ニ對シ通信交通
不能ノ為休戰命令下達ニ對シ
同線上北方ノ日本軍ニ援
持侯派遣一隅ニシ援助依賴セスリル

Japanese surrender leaflet dropped over southern Burma before official surrender aboard USS Missouri in Tokyo Bay.
Leaflet told all Japanese of the surrender and that their High Command instructed them to co-operate with the Allies, and obey the Allies instructions.

Pictured are: Lt/Gen Takazo Numata and R/Adml Kalgye Chudo

152 Squadron reunion in London
Len & Vicky seated far right

HW

TELEPHONE: Sloane 3467
~~XXXXXXXX~~

Extn............

Any communications on the
subject of this letter should
be addressed to:—
THE UNDER SECRETARY
OF STATE, AIR MINISTRY,
and the following number
quoted:— P.437433/S.14.Cas.B.2.

Your Ref................

AIR MINISTRY,
2, Seville Street,
LONDON, S.W.1.

14th December, 1948.

Sir,

I am directed to refer to the loss of your son, Flight
Lieutenant L.A. Smith, and to say that a full report of the
circumstances in which he lost his life has now been received,
and it is thought you would wish to have the available
information.

Your son, who was briefed to carry out an aerobatic
display in connection with the annual Battle of Britain
commemoration, took off from Leuchars airfield at 1.45 p.m.
on 18th September, 1948. After climbing to approximately
8,000 feet, he dived to 500 feet, following the dive with an
upward roll of two full turns. He dived back over the
airfield, climbed to 5,000 feet and again dived, this time
with the intention of doing a rocket loop. He levelled out
at 400 feet and appeared to be flying normally, when the
starboard wing was seen to fold backward and upward.
Various pieces then broke off the aircraft, which dived into
the ground and disintegrated. Your son must have been
killed instantly.

The primary cause of the accident, it is believed, was
the failure of the starboard main plane. The aircraft was
completely serviceable prior to the flight, and examination

/of

J.G. Smith, Esq.,
52, Hillingdon Street,
Walworth,
S.E.17.

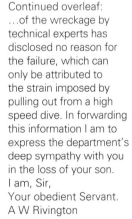

Continued overleaf:
...of the wreckage by
technical experts has
disclosed no reason for
the failure, which can
only be attributed to
the strain imposed by
pulling out from a high
speed dive. In forwarding
this information I am to
express the department's
deep sympathy with you
in the loss of your son.
I am, Sir,
Your obedient Servant.
A W Rivington

December Air Ministry crash report

Newspaper headlines after Len's tragic

Scots Girl Sees Fiance's Plane Fall

BANNS WERE TO HAVE BEEN CALLED TO-DAY

A 24-year-old St Andrews girl, Miss Mary Inglis, saw her fiance's plane crash ten minutes after the Battle of Britain air display began at Leuchars aerodrome yesterday afternoon.

Her fiance, 28-year-old Flight-Lieutenant, Leonard Alfred Smith, Norwood Avenue, Romford, Essex, was killed instantly when his Spitfire, the first to take the air for an aerobatics show, came to pieces 300 feet above the crowd.

The banns of their marriage, which was to have taken place on the first Saturday of next month, were to have been called at St Andrews to-day.

Their Last Chat

Seen at her home, 8 Market Street, St Andrews, Miss Inglis told a "Sunday Post" man she had been speaking to her fiance in his quarters before he left for the take off.

"He liked the idea of opening the display," she said. "and was his usual cheerful self.

"Something which had troubled but had not worried him was the fact that the Spitfire he should have flown crashed in a rehearsal during the week while being landed by another pilot.

"The Spitfire he flew to-day was a number 19, a heavier type."

Miss Inglis was taken home by car immediately after the accident.

Wing Falls Off

The Spitfire flown by Smith had done several aerobatic stunts before it failed to pull out of a power dive. It was first seen to be in difficulties right in front of the control tower.

Smoke began pouring from its engine, and the starboard wing fell off. Fragments of it showered down among a lone line of aircraft, and hundreds of people who were inspecting them.

A sea of upturned faces saw the aircraft continue east at 400 m.p.h., 200 feet up with smoke continuing to pour from it.

There was a minor explosion when it hit the ground about a quarter of a mile away, out of sight of spectators.

At the scene of the crash on the perimeter track wreckage was strewn around for several hundred yards. Only the engine could be recognised.

Fire Engine Mishap

On the way to the crashed plane the trailer of one fire engine became detached and crashed at a turn, but no one was injured.

After a hurried conference among high-ranking officers, the programme continued as planned. Minutes later, with the wreckage of the Spitfire scarcely burned out, the pilots of two Moths took off to do synchronised aerobatics. Thirteen other flying displays followed.

Flt.-Lieut. Smith had taken part in several air campaigns including the Battle of Britain. He was a holder of the D.F.M.

... IN EXILE

Daily Mirror

MON SEPT 20 1948

ONE PENNY

No. 13,955

Registered at G.P.O. as a Newspaper.

FORWARD WITH THE PEOPLE

...N GET THE

...S MINISTER:

...AN READY

...till produce the coal necessary to... output target promised by... with...ch Gaitskell, Fuel Minister.

£40...

Mr w the men can get the coal, it wa...ns secret until his meeting this... of the National Coal Board

extree...

three...

total...

£767...

final...

to ex...

Evans...

show...

and t...

was i...

A...

shoul...

anoth...

year...

val a...

write...

St...

askin...

sugge...

shoul...

If a...

comi...

as a...

life.

TH

A

"...

is ci...

allowed...

the Upr...

Brane...

who...

Serv...

purs...

ticul...

case

not'...

D.F.M. Killed In Exploding Spitfire

Receiving a telegram from Scotland on Saturday, Mrs. J. Rouse, of 86 Norwood-ave., Romford, expected it to contain a message about the wedding plans of her brother, Flt.-Lt. Leonard Alfred Smith. Instead it gave the news of his tragic death whilst flying his favourite 'plane, the Spitfire, in a Battle of Britain display—in full view of the girl he was to marry in only three weeks.

The incident was at Leuchars, Fife, and Flt.-Lt. Smith's 'plane was the first off the ground.

EXPLODED IN MID AIR

It was only 300 feet up, when, pulling from a power dive, it exploded in mid-air. Flt.-Lt. Smith, who was 28, had been in the R.A.F. since the beginning of the war, and made his home with Mrs. Rouse, his eldest sister and her husband, while on leave. "His whole life was in flying," Mrs. Rouse told the Romford Times, "and he could never look forward to have to leave the R.A.F." He had made many models of the "Spitty" for her, the 'plane in which he won the D.F.M. in Burma shortly before he was commissioned. He had 12 planes to his credit too.

His fiancee, Miss Mary Inglis, of 24 Market-street, St. Andrews, Fife, was watching the display. They were to have been married in three weeks, and Mrs. Rouse, who had never seen her, was planning a reception for them.

...CENHAM MAN

Mary Inglis.

Wished her pilot fiance "good luck," then saw him die in air explosion

Five minutes after wishing her fiance, Flight-Lieutenant Alfred Smith, 28, good luck in the aerobatic display he was about to give at Leuchars (Fife) RAF station on Saturday, Mary Inglis, 24, saw his Spitfire explode in mid-air, killing him.

Miss Inglis, who lives at Market-street, St. Andrews, said yesterday that the wedding had been postponed from the beginning of this month because of rehearsals for the display.

Flt.-Lieut. Smith.

◆

Death roll in the Manston RAF crash on Saturday, in which a Mosquito aircraft hit a line of cars, increased to twelve yesterday. Marie Allen, 21, of Merrick-square, The Borough, London, died in Margate Hospital. Her fiance, John Higgins, 25, gravely ... is not ...

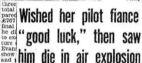

News columns from St Andrews Citizen & Romford Times papers.
Also featuring Daily Mirror front page headlines of Monday 20th September following the Saturday 18th September Battle of Britain Display

Ray in Calcutta - December 1943
Taken soon after arriving in India from
the Italian campaign

RAF Coningsby at the 60th anniversary of The Battle of Britain
Ray beside MK XIX Spitfire No PS915 from the Battle of Britain Memorial Flight
Painted in the livery of the Black Panther to honour 152 (Hyderabad) "F" Sqdn.

From the author, August 2011

After receiving the appraisal from Melrose for Birth of the Black Panthers I was delighted to forward a copy to Ray Johnson with the comment that publication was in all probability likely.

Ray was within one month of his ninety-first birthday, very frail and partially blind yet he was determined to phone me and felt elated when he discovered with the aid of his big numbered dial he actually made contact all by himself.

He phoned, he said, because he just needed to tell me that brother Len was the only Englishman to have won aerial combat against all three of our enemies whilst serving in the same squadron, and was prepared to challenge anyone who argued to the contrary.

I thanked him most warmly and declared that the number of achievements that now applied to my brother would be hard to put in written form without a certain public scepticism creeping in, however, I am pleased to report it.

Major Harry Hoffe, DFC
Armistice Day for SAAF
Edwards school in JHB
21st May 2011

11 Burn St
Waverley
2090
8th Dec 1997.

Dear Bill,

Many thanks for your letter
of 20 November enclosing the 1943
Baigachi menue, which revives many
happy memories of that period. Thank
you also for your Christmas and New
year wishes.

I must apologise for not replying
to your faxed letter of 10 June, but we
were staying at the coast for June
and July and when we got back
there was so much to be attended to
that it slipped my memory.

152 was the "Hyderabad Squadron"
sponsored by the Nizam of Hyderabad.
Whether there was any affiliation
between Hyderabad and Black Panthers
I do not know, but I do know that
the one that adorned the side of
our Spitfires was inspired and
executed by Smithy and Sergeant
Duval.

Pauline and I still enjoy
good health and busy lives after
fifteen years of retirement from

This letter is part of reply from Major Harry Hoffe, 152 Sqdn Commander who took over after loss of Bruce Ingham.
He writes in answer to my request for clarification on the adoption of the Black Panther insignia.
My understanding is that Duval first saw the image implanted on the nose of a Dakota, and brother Len showed his artistic impression superimposed on 152 Spits.

Duxford, 2006
William and Ernie Unstead

However, life carried on with patrols, escorts, attacking the marshaling yards at Mandalay, bombing the oilfields at Yen & Yong on the Irrawady etc etc, quite an hectic life, & gradualy I became accepted as one of the Sqdn especialy the comradship with W/O Partridge R.A.A.F. (Birdy)~ mad as a march hat & an advert for anybodies Booze !!. carried out several escorts for "Lord Louie Mountbatten" as one of a set group led by F/O Len Smith. I recall on one occasion scheduled to meet L/Mouutbattens silver Dakota at "Whites Cutting" coming from the Arakan at 05.00 Hrs to escort to "H.Q" up near the Chinese border. Got there & waited to no avail, Smithy decided to head for destination, H.Q.—Lo & behold there was the silver D.C. landed !!. It was the first & only time I heard smithy swear !!, when out of a nearby tent Lord Mountbatton appeared, he came straight up to Smithy & appologised for the upset & explained —we were early so I told the pilot to carry on, so it was my fault, we should have waited !!. That was a real mans Leadership, & after Smithy accepted the issue Lord "M" shook hands with us all.

Extract taken from W/O Ernie Unstead memoir.
Written by him for submission in 152 Hyderabad website
created by Robert Rooker on behalf of 152 Hyderabad F Squadron

Len's art saved by Ernie Unstead for over 60yrs
Drawn on a/c fabric

Ernie Unstead requested Smithy as Sqdn artist to produce a lifesize pin-up for the Sgts Mess at Tulihal. Then when he left took it, passing it to Teri when we all met at Duxford in 2006.

Ernie passed away the following year.

From left to right: Ray, G Hennah, Norman Jones and Norman Dear

Ray presenting the 152 Squadron badge and roll of honour to
S/Ldr Paul Day of The Battle of Britain Memorial Flight

**Panther Badge designed by
Len "Smithy" Smith**

Two sketches by Len given to Ron Patridge "Birdy" on his return to Australia as patterns for Squadron badge. These sketches passed to Robert Rooker by Ron's son Rowan. I contacted Rowan to ask of an aunt called Joy who Len wrote to. He replied in the affirmative, but said sadly both her and his Dad had died.

1998 – Duxford – "Flying Legends" Display
Mary & me Teri & Barry meet Ray for first time

Ray alongside Teri and Barry with Memphis Belle fortress as background

Enjoying the day. Bill, Mary, Ray and Barry

Millenium year 2000

At Ray's 80th birthday party in the gardens of his nephew's beautiful home near Grantham on the 4th September 2000

Mary gives Ray a hug on his 80th birthday

Mary and I smile at old photos of 152 with Norman Jones and Norman Dear.
Norman Dear on Mary's right tells her of the time Smithy emphasised a low flying discussion by flying his Spit so low he ran its tailwheel along the runway.

A nostalgic setting for Ray's 80th

The ladies all sang wartime favourites and the weather remained glorious throughout

Duxford 2006 - 152 pilot's line-up

Ray Johnson at right-hand end and Robert Rooker standing

152 pilots signing for customers

Ken Plumridge talks to Teri

Ernie Unstead partakes of a pint with Teri as they watch the display.
He had previously given Teri Len's drawing lovingly kept for 60 years.
Sadly Ernie passed away the following year.

Duxford 2006

Robert Rooker, founder of the 152 website, with his wife Elizabeth.
Robert kindly organised as many ex-152 pilots as possible to attend this, their special day.
Well done Rob and Liz.

Ray's 90th birthday party
Robert Rooker, Ray, Martin Johnston, William Smith.
Martin is son of Walter Johnston who served with 152 in 1941

Defined Types
Early Box Kite - Sopwith Camel - Gloucester Gladiator

April 9th 2002
Two Spitfires escort a Lancaster Bomber over The Mall. The day of the Queen Mother's Funeral.
One of the Spitfires, a MK XIX is in the livery of 152 Squadron complete with Black Panther.
This information is confirmed to me by none other than Ray Johnson

2012 W/O Eric Clegg 90yrs
ex-152 Squadron Black Panther pilot

2012 Major Harry Hoffe DFC 95yrs
ex-152 Squadron C/O
Black Panther pilot

**2012 Group Captain Gus
Ardeline DFC 95yrs**
ex-152 Squadron Black Panther pilot